IOWA WILDLIFE VIEWING GUIDE

ACKNOWLEDGMENTS

This viewing guide was the dream of the Iowa Department of Natural Resources' Wildlife Diversity Program. It was made a reality by the contributions of numerous conservation groups and individuals. The *Iowa Wildlife Viewing Guide* Steering Committee included the following people: Richard Bishop, Terry Little, Don Cummings, Laura Jackson, Lisa Hemesath, Ron Andrews, Bruce Ehresman, Pat Schlarbaum, Doug Harr, Doug Janke, Carl Priebe, Chuck Steffen, Dean Dalziel, Neil Heiser, Bob Moore, and Don Pfeiffer, from the Iowa Department of Natural Resources Wildlife Bureau; Dave Aplund, from the U.S. Fish and Wildlife Service, Walnut Creek Wildlife Refuge; Brenda Lackey, from the U.S. Corps of Engineers, Rock Island District; Darwin Koenig, from O'Brien County Conservation Board; Dennis Lewiston, from Jefferson County Conservation Board; and Miriam Patton, from Palo Alto County Conservation Board.

The committee was also supported by Larry Wilson, Director of the Iowa Department of Natural Resources, and the department's other divisions.

Nominations for sites were contributed by numerous county conservation boards, wildlife biologists, park rangers, foresters, and conservation groups. These also were gracious hosts who helped site reviewers Stephen J. Dinsmore, James J. Dinsmore, and Bruce L. Ehresman learn as much as possible about each area.

These local people also provided valuable comments on the first draft of their site description. They are invaluable links in helping visitors enjoy the sights of their area.

State Project Manager:
Laura Spess Jackson

Authors:
Stephen J. Dinsmore, Laura S. Jackson,
Bruce L. Ehresman, James J. Dinsmore

Wildlife Viewing Guide Program Manager
Kate Davies, Defenders of Wildlife

Illustrations
Jo Moore

Front cover photo
Eastern bluebird RICHARD DAY

Back cover photos
Wildflowers at Marietta Sand Prairie
State Preserve CARL KURTZ
Spicebush swallowtail CARL KURTZ

CONTENTS

REGION THREE: THE HEARTLAND

REGION FOUR: THE NORTHEAST PLATEAU

ADDITIONAL INFORMATION

Dinsmore, J.J. 1994. *A country so full of game: The story of wildlife in Iowa.* Univ. Iowa Press. 249 pp. Provides a historical perspective of the presence, distribution, extirpation and current status of species ranging from bison to shorebirds.

Iowa's County Conservation Boards. *Outdoor Adventure Guide* 1994. Iowa Association of County Conservation Boards. Box 79, Elkhart, IA 50073-0079 or local conservation board. 168 pp. Contains maps of each county, location of county conservation board areas and facilities.

Iowa Department of Natural Resources. Wallace State Office Building, Des Moines, IA 50319-0034. (515) 281-5145. Literature on state parks, forests, preserves, wildlife areas, various wildlife species, volunteer surveys, canoe access, boating, hunting, and fishing can be obtained.

Iowa Natural Heritage Foundation. 505 Fifth Avenue, Suite 444, Des Moines, IA 50309-2321. (515) 288-1846. *Trails for Iowa* guide.

Prior, J. C. 1991. *Landforms of Iowa.* Univ. Iowa Press. 153 pp. Very readable explanation of Iowa's geology and landforms.

Sportsman's Atlas. 1992. *Iowa sportsman's atlas: Back roads and outdoor recreation.* P.O. Box 132 Lytton, IA. 50561 107 pp. County by county map of all public areas in the state and local contact people.

Wolf, R. C. 1991. Iowa's state parks: Also forests, recreation areas and preserves. Iowa State Univ. Press. 212 pp. Book describing various public lands.

Published in cooperation with Defenders of Wildlife.

Design, typesetting, and other prepress work by Falcon Press, Helena, Montana.

Printed in Korea.

Cataloging-in-Publication Data

Jackson, Laura, 1957 Mar. 3-
Iowa wildlife viewing guide / Laura Jackson.
p. cm. --(Watchable wildlife series)
Includes bibliographical references and index.
ISBN 1-56044-349-9
1. Wildlife viewing sites--Iowa--Guidebooks. 2. Wildlife watching--Iowa--Guidebooks. 3. Iowa--Guidebooks I. Title. II. Series.
QL 176.J335 1995
591.9777--dc20 95-30819
CIP

PROJECT SPONSORS

The IOWA DEPARTMENT OF NATURAL RESOURCES is responsible for managing and protecting the state's fish, wildlife, energy, air, water, and geological resources. It also manages state parks, preserves, forests, and wildlife management areas. The IDNR is proud to sponsor this viewing guide and help people become more aware of the wonderful diversity of natural resources in Iowa. For additional information, contact the Iowa Department of Natural Resources, Wallace State Office Building, Des Moines, Iowa 50319-0034, (515) 281-5145.

DEFENDERS OF WILDLIFE is a national nonprofit organization of more than 100,000 members and supporters dedicated to preserving the natural abundance and diversity of wildlife and its habitat. A 1-year membership is $20 and includes subscriptions to *Defenders*, an award-winning conservation magazine, and *Wildlife Advocate*, an activist-oriented newsletter. To join, or for further information, write or call Defenders of Wildlife, 1101 14th Street NW, Suite 1400, Washington, DC 20005, (202) 682-9400.

RESOURCE ENHANCEMENT AND PROTECTION (REAP) PROGRAM is a long-term integrated effort to wisely use and protect Iowa's natural resources through the acquisition and management of public lands; the upgrading of public park and preserve facilities; environmental education, monitoring, and research. It encourages Iowans to develop a conservation ethic, and to make necessary changes in our activities to preserve a rich and diverse natural environment. For more information, contact the Iowa Department of Natural Resources.

The U.S. FISH AND WILDLIFE SERVICE is a proud sponsor of the *Iowa Wildlife Viewing Guide*. The agency has a mandate to conserve, protect, and enhance the nation's fish and wildlife resources and their habitats for the continuing benefit of the American people. Programs include management of migratory birds, freshwater fish, and anadromous fish, protection and recovery of endangered species, research, recreation/education, administration of the national wildlife refuge system, and law enforcement. For regional information, contact the U.S. Fish and Wildlife Service, Bishop Henry Whipple Federal Building, 1 Federal Drive, Fort Snelling, Minnesota 55111-4056, (612) 725-3313.

The NATIONAL FISH AND WILDLIFE FOUNDATION is chartered by Congress to stimulate private giving to conservation and is an independent not-for-profit organization. It helped stimulate Partnerships for Wildlife challenge grants, which forged partnerships between public and private sectors to produce this guide and similar projects conserving the nation's fish, wildlife, and plants. National Fish and Wildlife Foundation, Bender Building, 1120 Connecticut Avenue NW Suite 900, Washington, DC 20036, (202) 857-0166.

The U.S. ARMY CORPS OF ENGINEERS, Rock Island District, plans, designs, builds, and manages water resources and other civil works projects in cooperation with other federal, state, and local sponsors. These activities include flood protection, navigation channel and harbor improvements and maintenance, and regulatory and real estate functions. In Iowa the Corps manages 4 major flood control reservoirs and navigation along the Mississippi and Missouri rivers. The Rock Island District has been a co-sponsor of major wildlife educational programs in its region and is proud to promote further awareness of the nation's natural resources by its sponsorship of Iowa's Watchable Wildlife initiative. For additional information contact U.S. Army Corps of Engineers, Rock Island District, Mississippi River Visitor Center, Clock Tower Bldg., P.O. Box 2004, Rock Island, IL 61204-2004; phone (309) 794-5338.

The IOWA ORNITHOLOGISTS' UNION, founded in 1923, encourages interest in the identification, study, and protection of birds in Iowa and seeks to unite those who share these interests. The group maintains the Iowa Birdline birding hotline, and publishes *Iowa Bird Life*, *I.O.U. News*, and other educational material. Memberships cost $15 and include quarterly publications. For additional information, contact the Iowa Ornithologists' Union, 4024 Arkansas Drive, Ames, Iowa 50014.

IOWA CHAPTER, THE WILDLIFE SOCIETY is a professional society of wildlife biologists, educators, and administrators. The organization uses its expertise to comment on environmental legislation and provide continuing education for its members and others concerned about management of Iowa resources. The Iowa Chapter is also involved in national wildlife-oriented issues through its connection with The Wildlife Society. It produces a newsletter and annually hosts at least 1 educational workshop. Iowa Wildlife Society, 1436 255th Street, Boone, Iowa 50036, (515) 432-2823.

DEPARTMENT OF DEFENSE (DOD) is the steward of about 25 million acres of land in the United States, many of which possess irreplaceable natural and cultural resources. The DOD is pleased to support the Watchable Wildlife Program through its Legacy Resource Management Program, a special initiative to enhance the conservation and restoration of natural and cultural resources on military land. For more information contact the Office of the Deputy Under Secretary of Defense (Environmental Security), 400 Navy Drive, Suite 206, Arlington, VA 22202-2884.

IMPORTANT CONTRIBUTORS

Iowa Raptor Foundation

Iowa Audubon Council

Iowa Conservation Education Council, Inc.

Iowa Association of Naturalists

Fort Dodge Izaak Walton League

Webster County Conservation Foundation

Ottumwa Bird Club

Dubuque Audubon Society

Northern Iowa Prairie lakes Audubon Society

Des Moines Izaak Walton League

Burlington Bank and Trust

INTRODUCTION

Native Americans referred to Iowa as "the beautiful land." Although the state is now deceptively cloaked in seemingly uniform agricultural fields, and regularly broken by small towns or sprawling urban areas, Iowa is a diverse biological crossroads.

Many animals and plants meet the north-south and east-west limits of their range in Iowa. Hence the state is home to both eastern and western kingbirds; plains spadefoot toads in the west and spring peeper frogs in the east; pecan trees in the south and white pines in the north; and a host of other combinations. Historically, about 80 percent of Iowa's landscape was covered by a mosaic of tallgrass and wetland prairies. Trees were largely confined to the river valleys and associated uplands. With the exception of bottomland forests, many woodlands were open savannahs, kept free of dense understory by climatic conditions, browsing by elk and bison, which once roamed the state, and frequent fires caused naturally or set by native people. The prairie plants, with their dense, 6-foot root systems, created some of the most fertile soil in the world. Consequently, more than 90 percent of Iowa's landscape has been converted to farmlands vital to the country's food and energy production.

The 77 sites featured in this book will help you explore some of Iowa's remaining natural areas. Floating along the wooded bluffs and canyons of the Upper Iowa River, observing thousands of snow geese in the Missouri River Valley, listening to the songbirds along a forest trail, or watching butterflies dancing among prairie flowers, you will find that Iowa has much to offer. As you view a bald eagle clutching a fish, pelicans gathered on a sandbar, or a river otter slipping through the water, remember that wildlife needs your support. Consult the selected reading list to further investigate the state's natural treasures, or join one of the groups listed as a sponsor to learn more about the state's wildlife. Take part, and do what you can do to ensure Iowa's wild future.

THE NATIONAL WATCHABLE WILDLIFE PROGRAM

Wildlife recreation is one of our nation's most popular outdoor activities. In Iowa, more than 80 percent of adults enjoy viewing, feeding, or photographing the state's wildlife, and more than $332 million is spent annually by these people on wildlife recreation not associated with hunting (Gallup, 1994).

Unlike hunters and anglers, who pay for wildlife enhancement programs through license fees and taxes on equipment, less than 2 percent of non-hunting wildlife viewers pay for statewide programs. For years, non-game species benefited from dollars generated by hunters, since they often shared land that was acquired and managed for hunting. But now, with increasing demand for wildlife viewing, there is a vital need for management of watchable species and more habitat protection. Efforts are underway to increase funding for watchable wildlife programs at both state and national levels. The money generated would allow better protection of our nation's wildlife and prevent population declines in the 80 percent of the state's wildlife that is not hunted.

The National Watchable Wildlife Program is a catalyst of this effort. Founded in 1990 with the idea of bridging the gap between federal agencies, states, hunters, and non-hunters, the program was established to provide people with the opportunity to view wildlife and gain a better appreciation of the diversity of natural habitats needed to preserve our wildlife heritage. A state-by-state series of wildlife viewing guides will lay the foundation for the program.

This *Iowa Wildlife Viewing Guide* represents the first step of a long-term commitment to protect the state's natural areas and foster a better appreciation of wildlife. The binoculars logo that appears on all National Watchable Wildlife Program signs will be used in our state, to help visitors locate viewing sites. At this time, not all areas are marked with signs. As state and federal funding initiatives pass, additional signs, trails, interpretive facilities, and educational programs will be developed, and current sites will be improved.

Today, some wildlife viewing areas have nearby visitor centers or offices where maps and additional information can be acquired. Other areas have only a parking lot from which visitors have to forge their own trails to explore the area. In either case, the experience of viewing wildlife is one that cannot be duplicated. Enjoy Iowa's diverse Watchable Wildlife!

WILDLIFE VIEWING TIPS

Wildlife viewing is often seasonal. Learn enough about the life history of wildlife to know when the species you seek is most active, and whether it migrates or is present year-round in the state. The Wildlife Index in this guide highlights the best viewing sites for some species.

When possible, call ahead to a viewing site, since local conditions and weather can affect viewing. For birds, the I.O.U. Birdline provides weekly updates on viewing. Currently, the phone number is (319) 338-9881.

Here are some more tips that will held you look for wildlife in Iowa:

The early bird catches the worm. This is more than just a saying. Wildlife tends to be most active around sunrise and sunset. During summer, many species hide from midday heat. During winter, the opposite may be true—some species become more active as the day warms.

Enjoy a wild nightlife. Although you may not be able to see wildlife after dark, you can enjoy the hooting of owls at night during late winter or early spring. During summer, you may want to take in a chorus of frogs while fireflies flicker around you.

Learn to hide. The best viewing often comes when you are concealed. Vehicles and boats can double as blinds. Portable blinds, or even camouflage material used as a cloak, can enhance viewing. Be sure to sit quietly.

Stop-look-listen. Move slowly as you walk through an area, and stop frequently. Slow movement helps prevent startling wildlife; stopping helps wildlife resume normal activities. Learn to listen for wildlife. Many species become obvious when you let them tell you their location.

View wildlife from a distance. Use binoculars, spotting scopes, or telephoto lenses to view wildlife. This will enhance the details, and you can observe wild creatures while reducing the likelihood of disturbing them.

Practice stress reduction. If you see an animal is becoming nervous—tapping its foot, bobbing its head, or raising its wings for flight—retreat. Repeated flushing or scaring of wildlife can force these animals to use valuable calories. Wildlife needs all its energy to raise its young, survive a dry summer or cold winter's night, and successfully migrate.

Respect privacy. Wildlife needs an undisturbed environment to successfully rear young. Avoid disturbing nest and den sites, and leave baby animals at their natural homes. Also avoid excessive use of recordings to lure animals to you. Many tapes imitate a territorial animal, and the animal you want to see can be scared away or exhausted by continually trying to defend it's territory against a fake intruder.

Play detective. Arm yourself with field guides on both plants and animals. Since wildlife is often secretive, learn to read tracks and other signs. Even though you might not have seen it, you can enjoy knowing that an otter, beaver, deer, or wild turkey crossed the creek or trail before you.

Relax. Allow yourself enough time to take full advantage of wildlife viewing opportunities. Wildlife lives by daily and seasonal timetables—not hourly deadlines. Consequently, viewing takes time, patience, a relaxed pace, and a little luck.

Be prepared. Not all sites have facilities, so always carry water, a snack, a small first-aid kit, and appropriate clothing when you journey outdoors. Use insect repellent and tuck your pant legs into your boots as you walk outside; upon returning from the field, carefully check yourself and others for ticks. Although not as prevalent as it is in some other states, Lyme disease has been reported in Iowa.

Improve the area. Help create better habitat for wildlife by picking up trash, reporting vandalism, and teaching others about the experiences you enjoyed.

HOW TO USE THIS GUIDE

Your wildlife viewing guide contains a wealth of information. Please take a few moments to become familiar with its contents and organization.

Iowa is divided into **4 viewing regions** that correspond with **color-coded page margins** for quick access. The guide begins with Region 1, the westernmost Loess Hills region, then moves north and eastward to Regions 2 and 3, the Prairie Pothole and Heartland parts of the state. It concludes in the Northeast Plateau with Region 4. Each regional section begins with photographs and information about the region, a **regional map**, a **list of viewing sites**, and artwork depicting major watchable species.

The viewing sites are numbered and listed with the site name. The site **description** provides a general overview of the area's habitats, and names species likely to be encountered in each type of habitat. The **viewing information** section provides more specific information on viewing, and gives the best times and seasons for observing some species. *NOTES OF CAUTION REGARDING ROAD CONDITIONS, VIEWING LIMITATIONS, AND OTHER RESTRICTIONS OR PRECAUTIONS APPEAR IN CAPITAL LETTERS.*

Written **directions** are supplied for each viewing site. The **size** of the site and name of the **closest town** appear beneath these. The closest town **usually** has gas, food and often lodging, but in Iowa you are seldom far from these amenities. Plan to supplement this information with an updated highway map, county map, or atlas. Watch for viewing site signs portraying the brown-and-white binoculars logo, and for state park, wildlife management area, boat ramp, or other brown highway signs to guide your approach. **Site ownership** and **phone numbers** are provided to help you acquire additional information prior to your visit. **Icons** representing available facilities and other recreational opportunities are provided at the end of each site description.

SITE OWNER/MANAGER ABBREVIATIONS

IDNR	Iowa Department of Natural Resources
CCB	County Conservation Board
USFWS	U.S. Fish and Wildlife Service
USACOE	U.S. Army Corps of Engineers
NPS	National Park Service
TNC	The Nature Conservancy

IOWA

Wildlife Viewing Areas

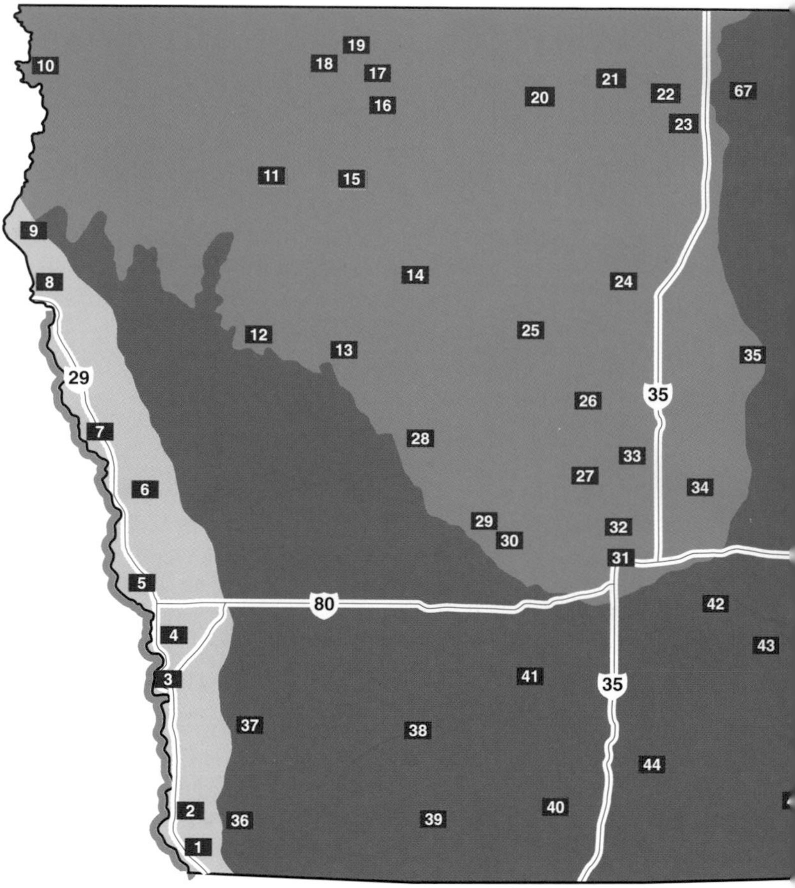

HIGHWAY SIGNS

As you travel in Iowa and other states, look for these special highway signs that identify wildlife viewing sites. These signs will help guide you to the viewing area. NOTE: Be sure to read the written directions provided with each site in this book—highway signs may refer to more than one site along a particular route.

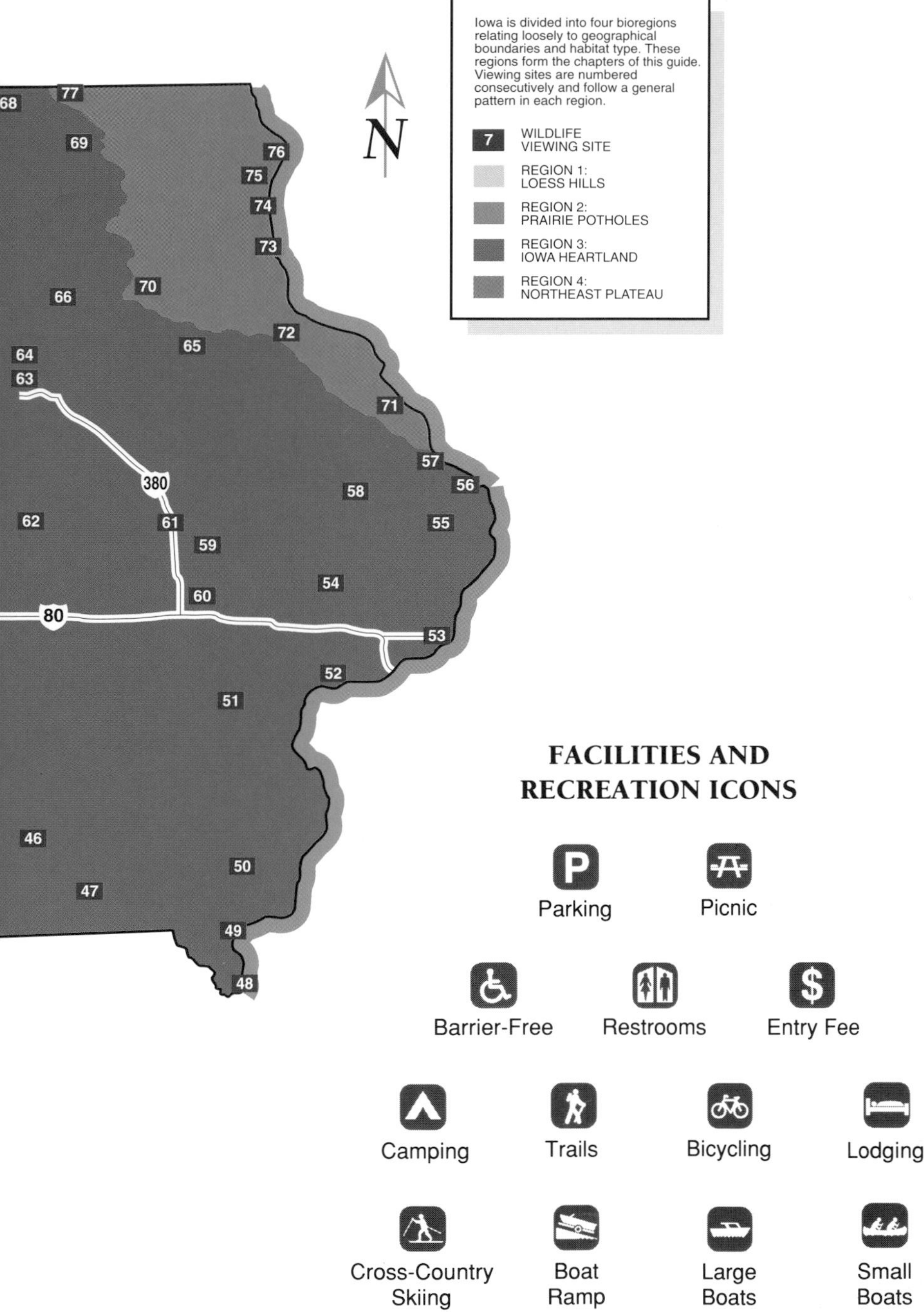
Iowa is divided into four bioregions relating loosely to geographical boundaries and habitat type. These regions form the chapters of this guide. Viewing sites are numbered consecutively and follow a general pattern in each region.
7 WILDLIFE VIEWING SITE
REGION 1: LOESS HILLS
REGION 2: PRAIRIE POTHOLES
REGION 3: IOWA HEARTLAND
REGION 4: NORTHEAST PLATEAU
N
380
80
46 47 48 49 50 51 52 53 54 55 56 57 58 59 60 61 62 63 64 65 66 68 69 70 71 72 73 74 75 76 77
FACILITIES AND RECREATION ICONS
Parking
Picnic
Barrier-Free
Restrooms
Entry Fee
Camping
Trails
Bicycling
Lodging
Cross-Country Skiing
Boat Ramp
Large Boats
Small Boats

REGION ONE: THE LOESS HILLS

The Loess Hills region of Iowa includes the Missouri River Alluvial Plain and forms a relatively narrow band, 200 miles long, on the western border of the state. The alluvial plain was formed by glacial melt water that eventually formed the Missouri River floodplain. Silt from the floodplain was blown eastward by the wind and deposited as a series of steep, irregular ridges that jut like mountains above the flat floodplain. Iowa's steep loess ridges are unique landforms, found elsewhere only in China.

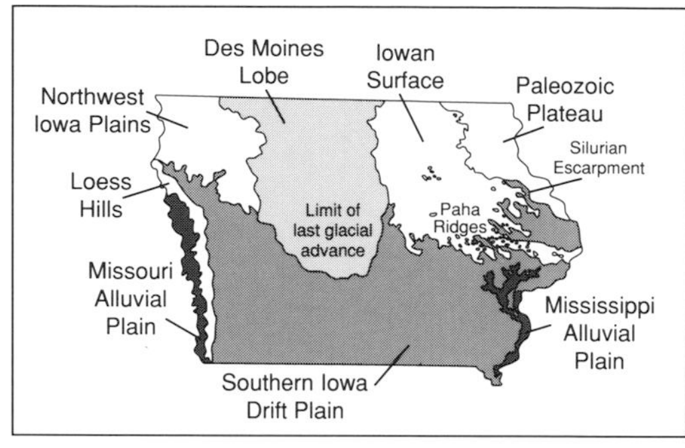

The floodplain in Region 1 was once an extensive prairie wetland with a network of river channels, sandbars, and the occasional cottonwood stand. Explorers Meriwether Lewis and William Clark journeyed up the Missouri River in 1804 and marveled at the abundant fish and wildlife along its course. Work to contain the Missouri River in a permanent channel was begun in 1882, and today 67 percent of this, our nation's longest river, is channeled or impounded.

Prairie fires, caused naturally or set by Native Americans, scorched the loess ridges and kept the hills nearly treeless until 150 years ago. The hills, with their dry, almost desert-like microhabitats, supported plants more typical of regions hundreds of miles to the west, such as yucca and prickly pear cactus. Trees are gradually invading the fire-starved ridges and slowly covering the prairies with woodlands. More than 10,000 acres of the Loess Hills have been designated a National Natural Landmark by the U.S. Department of the Interior.

The floodplains and hills are rich in wildlife. A million or more snow geese migrate through the area each fall, forming spectacular concentrations at sites such as DeSoto National Wildlife Refuge. Species more common farther west, such as the western kingbird, lark sparrow, plains spadefoot toad, prairie skink, and plains pocket mouse, can also be found in this region. Careful observations at prairie viewing sites can reveal some rare butterflies.

Loess Hills. DON POGGENSEE

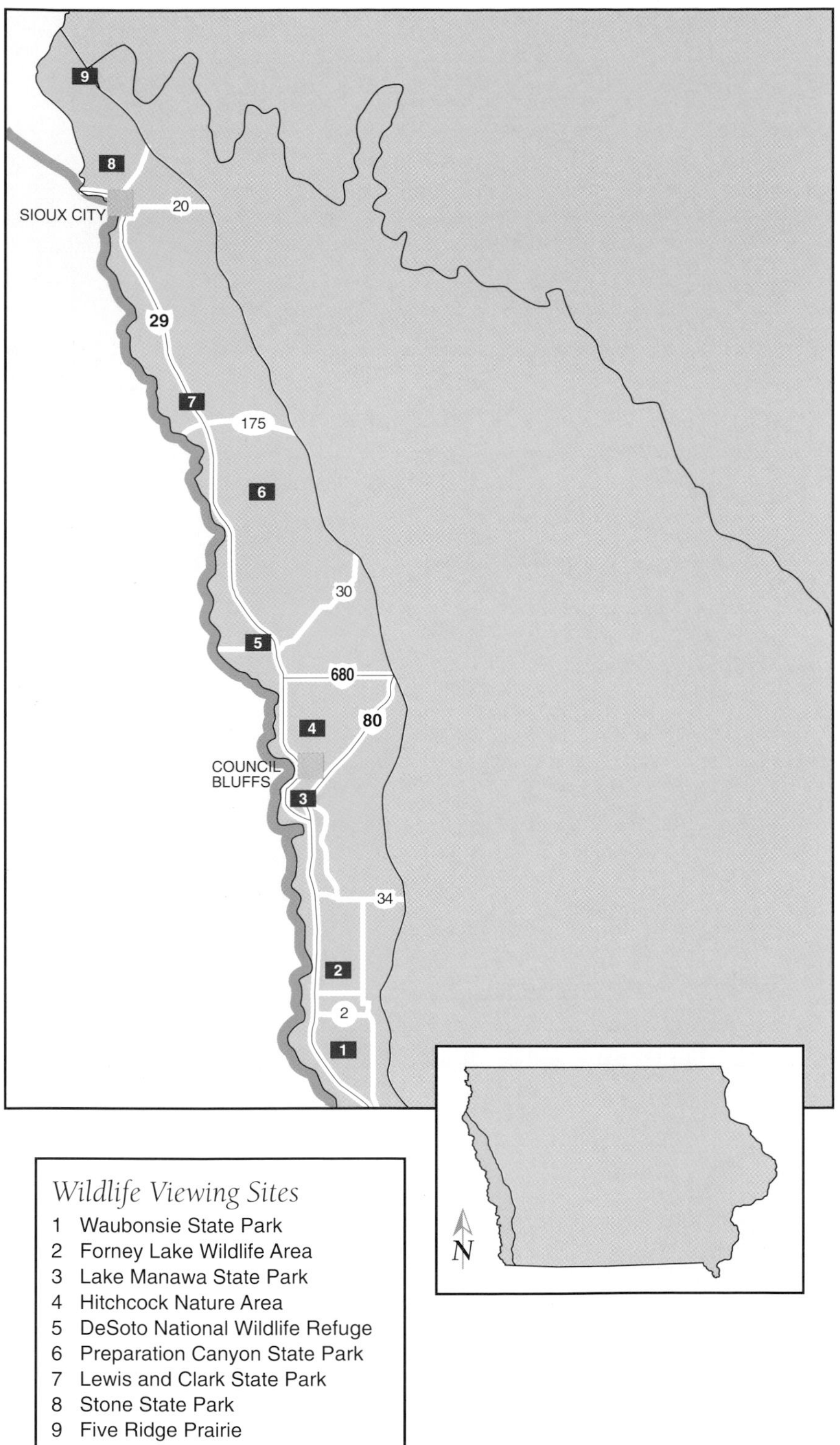
9
8
SIOUX CITY
20
29
7
175
6
30
5
680
4
80
COUNCIL BLUFFS
3
34
2
2
1
N
Wildlife Viewing Sites
1 Waubonsie State Park
2 Forney Lake Wildlife Area
3 Lake Manawa State Park
4 Hitchcock Nature Area
5 DeSoto National Wildlife Refuge
6 Preparation Canyon State Park
7 Lewis and Clark State Park
8 Stone State Park
9 Five Ridge Prairie

EAST MEETS WEST: LANDFORMS OF WIND

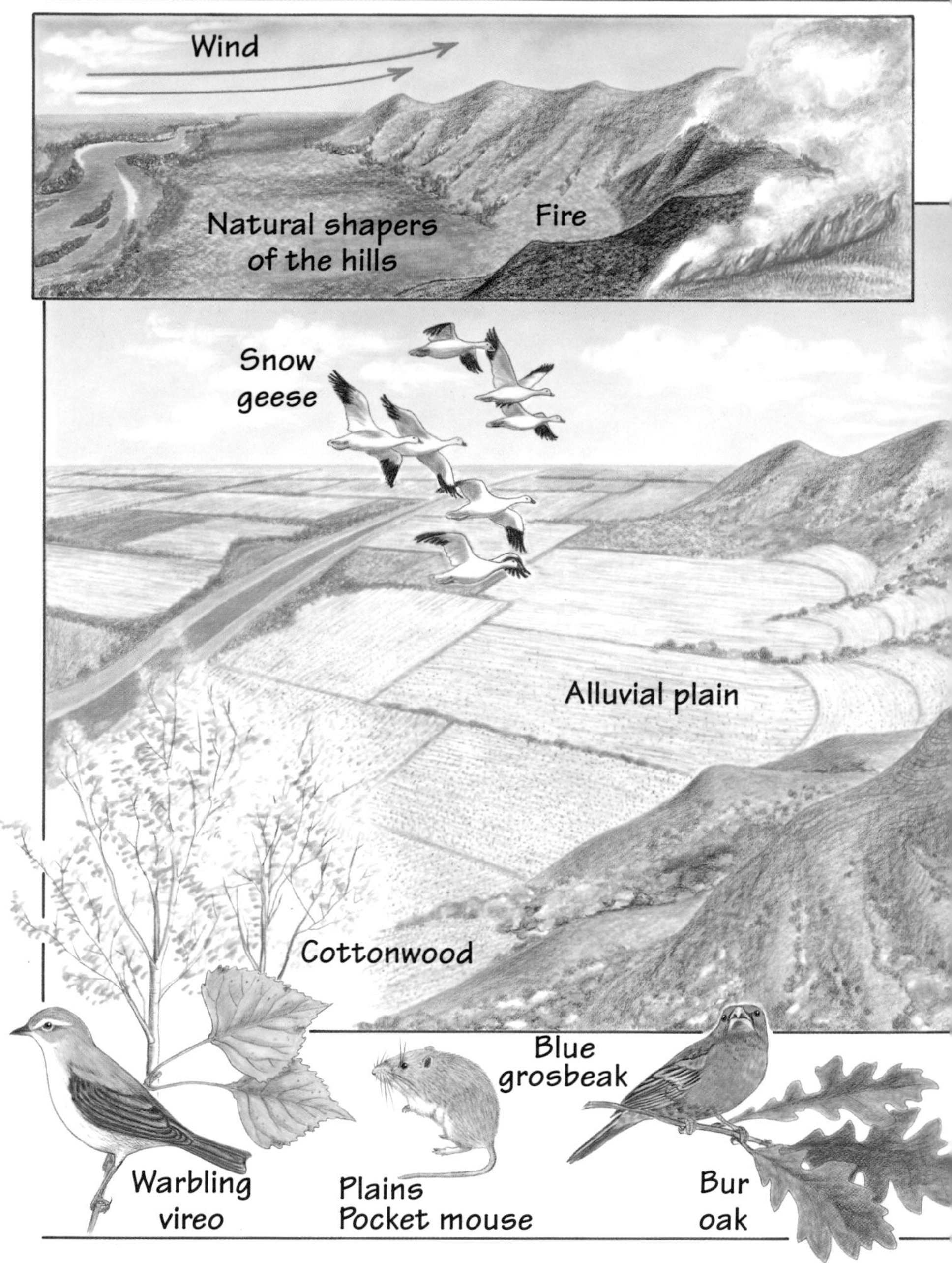

The restless meandering of the Missouri River has been largely confined to a narrow channel, allowing its flat floodplain to be converted to fields of corn and soybeans. Rising above the valley are the steep, irregular ridges of the Loess Hills, created by the deposition of wind-blown silt. For the last 150 years, as fire has been suppressed, bur oaks and red cedars have invaded the once nearly treeless hills. Midgrass prairies with little

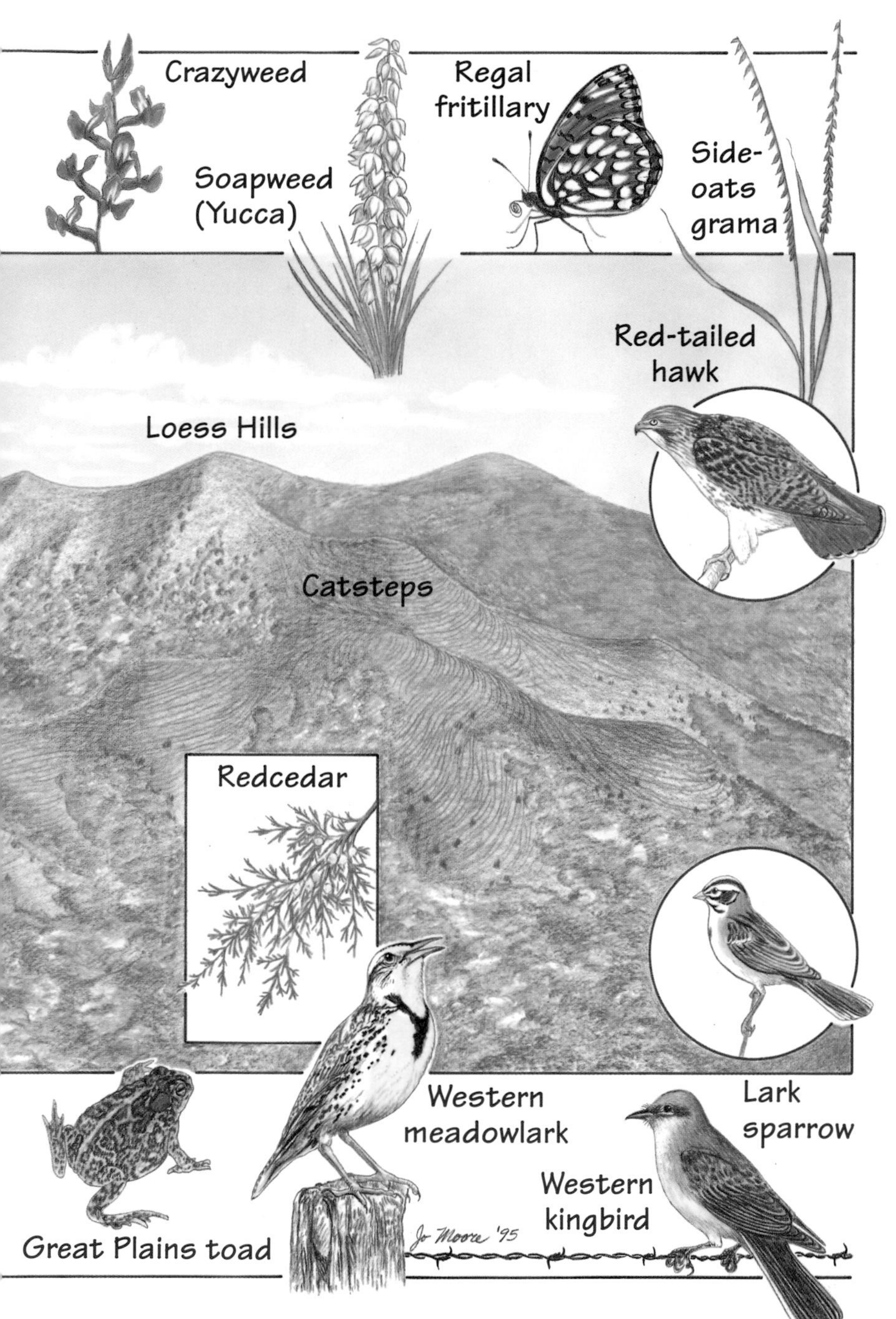

bluestem, sideoats grama, skeletonweed, and yucca are still found in the region. Lark sparrows can be seen in brushy areas near the loess ridges and grasslands, while blue grosbeaks favor the farmlands of the valley. Several species of western toads can be heard singing in the region, too. Thousands of snow geese and waterfowl migrate through the area. Sites 1, 4, and 6 treat visitors to panoramic views of the Loess Hills.

1. WAUBONSIE STATE PARK

Description: This park in the scenic Loess Hills consists of oak-covered bluffs with steep ravines and views of the Missouri River valley. Mammals seen at the site include white-tailed deer, bobcats, red foxes, and several species of bats. Nesting birds include broad-winged hawks, wild turkeys, whip-poor-wills, ovenbirds, Louisiana waterthrushes, Kentucky warblers, and summer and scarlet tanagers. The park is excellent for migrant thrushes, warblers, and sparrows. It is also home to northern prairie skinks and prairie racerunners.

Viewing Information: The park contains more than 7 miles of trails. The Ridge and Sunset Ridge Interpretive Trails offer scenic views of the Loess Hills and Missouri River valley. The overlook at Ridge Trail is also a good spot to view migrant raptors from September through October, and to see turkey vultures in summer. Summer and scarlet tanagers breed near the campground. Blue-gray gnatcatchers are common breeders along the Picnic Area Trail. On summer evenings, listen for whip-poor-wills and barred owls. Chuck-will's-widows breed in the bluffs just north of the park. Wild turkeys and white-tailed deer are common and often are seen along park roads and trails.

Directions: *From Sidney, follow Iowa Highway 2/U.S. Highway 275 south for 4.2 miles, then turn west on IA 2. Proceed 2 miles and turn south on Iowa Highway 239. Proceed south 0.4 mile to the park entrance. Obtain a map at the park office.*

Ownership: IDNR (712) 382-2786

Size: 1,247 acres

Closest Town: Sidney

The ovenbird's distinctive call of "tea-cher tea-cher tea-cher" is easily recognized. In larger forests such as Waubonsie State Park, this bird constructs a domed nest on the ground; the finished nest resembles a miniature Dutch oven. TODD FINK

2. FORNEY LAKE WILDLIFE AREA

Description: Located in the Missouri River valley below the Loess Hills, this natural marsh is known for its concentrations of snow geese and other waterfowl. Concentrations of up to 100 bald eagles have been noted here. Nesting birds include pied-billed grebes, least bitterns, common moorhens, marsh wrens, yellow-headed blackbirds, and occasionally a few great-tailed grackles. Muskrats and white-tailed deer are residents.

Viewing Information: The best viewing is from the gravel road along the south side of the area. Park in one of the pullouts, especially near hunting blinds 21-23. A canoe might be helpful in spring and early summer. Peak waterfowl numbers are present in March when concentrations of 50,000 or more snow geese are present. Peak numbers of bald eagles occur at this time and are best seen roosting in the large cottonwood trees at the east end of the marsh. In spring, listen for plains spadefoot toads, as well as the more common American toad and leopard frog. American white pelicans can be seen here from April through May and from August through September. In late summer, look for egrets and night-herons, especially as they fly into the marsh at dusk to roost. Viewing during fall is not possible since parking along the gravel road south of the marsh is prohibited. The 366-acre tract south of the gravel road near the west edge of the marsh contains borrow pits and shelterbelts. Waterfowl use the barrow pits from March through April, and the shelterbelts are home to nesting Bell's vireos. *FROM SEPTEMBER 15 THROUGH DECEMBER 25, MUCH OF THE AREA IS CLOSED FOR WATERFOWL HUNTING.*

Directions: *From Interstate 29, take the Bartlett exit (Exit 24). Proceed east 0.1 mile on County Road L31 and turn south (still on CR L31). Proceed 2.8 miles and turn east on a gravel road. After 0.6 mile the marsh is visible to the north.*

Ownership: IDNR (712) 374-3133

Size: 1,297 acres

Closest Town: Thurman

More than 390 bird species have been observed in Iowa. Nearly 200 species nest in the state, but 73 species dominate the state's avifauna.

3. LAKE MANAWA STATE PARK

Description: On the south side of Council Bluffs, Lake Manawa was once an oxbow bend of the nearby Missouri River. The lake hosts large numbers of waterfowl during migration; 20 or more species may be seen in a day. Loons, grebes, cormorants, gulls, and terns frequent the area in migration. This is an excellent area to see bald eagles, with concentrations of up to 50 or more noted. White-tailed deer and raccoons are common along the lake.

Viewing Information: The best view of the lake is from the boat ramp along the south side of the lake, north of the beach. Arrive early in the morning for the best light (and also to beat the boats to the lake). Look for waterfowl and other aquatic birds from March through April and from October through November. Bald eagles are easily seen in March and from November to freeze-up. In March, listen for American woodcock in grassy openings along the south side of the lake. Large numbers of cormorants gather on the lake in April and October and roost in the cottonwoods at the south end of the lake. American white pelican flocks are present in April. Look for painted turtles sunning themselves on logs in the canal to the west of the road on the western edge of the lake. Tree swallows, eastern bluebirds, and Bell's vireos are common nesters along the south side of the lake. White-tailed deer are residents as well.

Directions: *From Interstate 29 in Council Bluffs, take the Iowa Highway 92/U.S. Highway 275 exit (Exit 47). Follow IA 92/US 275 west 1.5 miles and turn south on South 11th Street. Proceed 0.1 mile to the park entrance. Bear right on Shore Drive and follow signs to the park office for a park map.*

Ownership: IDNR (712) 366-0220

Size: 1,529 acres

Closest Town: Council Bluffs

More than 125 butterfly species have been observed in Iowa. Seventy of those species use prairies, and 20 species are indicative of healthy, intact prairies. Butterflies can be attracted to your backyard by growing plants from the daisy, carrot, and milkweed families.

4. HITCHCOCK NATURE AREA

Description: This area in the Loess Hills consists of oak-hickory forest with some remnant Loess Hills prairie. There are spectacular views looking west over the Missouri River floodplain, making this a favorite site for hawk watchers. White-tailed deer, coyotes, red foxes, woodchucks, and wild turkeys are residents here. Nesting birds include whip-poor-wills, wood thrushes, gray catbirds, rufous-sided towhees, and northern orioles.

Viewing Information: Watch for 14 species of migrant raptors from the deck of Hitchcock's Lodge from September through October, including sharp-shinned, broad-winged, and red-tailed hawks. Lucky watchers might see a golden eagle in October. Walk the trails to see migrant warblers and sparrows. In winter, check the feeders around the lodge for winter resident birds such as white-breasted nuthatches and purple finches, as well as fox squirrels. Red foxes are frequently seen in the area.

Directions: *From Interstate 29 north of Council Bluffs, take the Crescent exit (Exit 61A). Follow Iowa Highway 988 east 2.2 miles to Iowa Highway 183. Proceed north 4.5 miles on IA 183 and turn west on Page Lane. Proceed 0.2 mile and turn north on Ski Hill Loop. Proceed 0.3 mile to the entrance to the area, on the left.*

Ownership: Pottawattamie County Conservation Board (712) 328-5638

Size: 582 acres

Closest Town: Crescent

Red fox pups are usually born in March. By late spring, the young emerge from their den and may be seen frolicking nearby. ROGER A. HILL

5. DESOTO NATIONAL WILDLIFE REFUGE

Description: This large oxbow of the Missouri River hosts spectacular numbers of snow geese and other waterfowl each fall. Up to 500,000 snow geese may be present at the peak season. Puddle ducks are commonly seen here, especially mallards, gadwalls, northern shovelers, and green-winged teal. The refuge also attracts fall concentrations of bald eagles, sometimes numbering 50 or more. The floodplain forest is home to white-tailed deer, wild turkeys, northern bobwhites, and woodpeckers year-round. Nesting birds include wood ducks, green herons, red-headed woodpeckers, sedge wrens, American redstarts, and lark sparrows. Yellow-headed blackbirds nest on the refuge and at nearby Noble's Lake. Coyotes and red foxes are residents.

Viewing Information: The peak time to visit is November, when large numbers of snow geese are present. Late November is generally best, though the best time varies depending on weather. Early morning and mid-afternoon are the most favorable times to see snow geese. Viewing is from the visitor center (open 9 a.m. - 4:30 p.m. daily) or the observation platform at the end of the Auto Tour (open October 15 through November 30). Coyotes are often seen feeding on injured geese, especially in fields north of the visitor center and across the lake from the observation platform. Scan the large goose flocks for greater white-fronted, Ross's, and Canada geese. Peak numbers of ducks are present in October and November, with the majority being mallards. Small numbers of most other common ducks can be found. Bald eagles perch in cottonwoods along the oxbow, but are best seen from the observation platform or the visitor center. Waterfowl migration is also good from March through April, but very few snow geese use the area at this time. White-tailed deer and wild turkeys are commonly seen along wooded edges within the refuge. Be sure to see the displays about the historic steamboat *bertrand. FOR THE BENEFIT OF THE GEESE AND MIGRATORY BIRDS, PLEASE STAY OUT OF CLOSED AREAS.*

***Directions:** From Interstate 29, take the Missouri Valley exit (Exit 75). Follow U.S. Highway 30 west 5.7 miles to the refuge entrance, on the left.*

Ownership: USFWS (712) 642-4121

Size: 7,823 acres

Closest Town: Missouri Valley

6. PREPARATION CANYON STATE PARK

Description: Nestled among the scenic Loess Hills in west-central Iowa, this park is largely undeveloped, making it a haven for wildlife. Much of the park is composed of oak forest, though there are several small remnant prairies at the east end of the area. Nesting birds here include turkey vultures, northern bobwhites, eastern wood-pewees, eastern bluebirds, ovenbirds, Kentucky warblers, and scarlet tanagers. Wild turkeys, white-tailed deer, red and gray foxes, coyotes, and woodchucks also live here. Bats can be seen during summer.

Viewing Information: More than 3 miles of trails traverse the park. Nesting birds, such as ovenbirds and Kentucky warblers, are found along the creek in the eastern portion of the park. Turkey vultures often ride thermals on the bluffs surrounding the park in summer. Wild turkeys are commonly seen along park roads, as are white-tailed deer and an occasional red or gray fox. The Loess Hills Pioneer State Forest lies adjacent to the southern boundary of the park. The wildlife of that area is similar to that found in the park; the forest also contains open habitats that attract nesting rufous-sided towhees and field and lark sparrows.

Directions: *From the junction of Iowa Highway 183 and County Roads E54 and L16 in Moorhead, follow IA 183 southwest for 2.2 miles and turn north on a paved road. Proceed 2.3 miles to the park entrance, on the left. Park maps are available at the kiosk at the park entrance.*

Ownership: IDNR (712) 423-2829

Size: 344 acres

Closest Town: Moorhead

More than 1 million snow geese migrate through western Iowa each fall. Thousands of geese may be observed at DeSoto National Wildlife Refuge during the peak of migration (see opposite page).
DON POGGENSEE

One of Iowa's most strikingly colored species, the rose-breasted grosbeak winters from Mexico to South America and nests in woodlands across the state. Its lengthy song resembles the robin's. JOHN HEIDECKER

7. LEWIS AND CLARK STATE PARK

Description: The park lies inside Blue Lake, a 650-acre oxbow lake and marsh on the Missouri River. It was named after the Lewis and Clark expedition, a corps of discovery sent out by President Thomas Jefferson, which stopped here in 1804. Much of the park is bottomland forest dominated by large cottonwoods and silver maples. Nesting birds here include wood ducks, red-headed woodpeckers, eastern bluebirds, warbling vireos, rose-breasted grosbeaks, and northern orioles. Mammals in the park include white-tailed deer, muskrats, beavers, and red foxes. Blue Lake offers a variety of habitats, including a large lake and cattail marsh.

Viewing Information: A 1-mile, self-guided nature trail and several other hiking trails provide access to wooded areas within the park. Watch for white-tailed deer along park roads at dusk. Ducks and geese abound on Blue Lake during migration, with Canada geese, wood ducks, and mallards nesting here. A few Canada geese and other waterfowl may winter on the aerated portion of the lake. Bald eagles occasionally perch in the large cottonwoods along the lake in March and November. American white pelicans show up regularly during migration. A variety of shorebirds, herons, egrets, rails, common moorhens, terns, yellow warblers, and yellow-headed blackbirds are regulars from spring to fall on marshy areas of Blue Lake, especially in the southeast portion, south of Iowa Highway 175. During spring and early summer, American toads are common here and easily heard.

Directions: *From Interstate 29 take the Onawa exit (Exit 112). Proceed west on Iowa Highway 175 for 1.4 miles and turn north at the entrance to the park. A map of the area is available at the park office.*

Ownership: IDNR (712) 423-2829

Size: 176 acres (plus a 230-acre lake)

Closest Town: Onawa

Iowa has 8 species of bats. Bats can eat nearly 600 insects per hour and are an important factor in controlling insect populations. Globally, bat-pollinated plants produce more than 450 human-used products ranging from bananas, cashews, and tequila, to medicines, fiber, fuel and fodder.

8. STONE STATE PARK

Description: Stone State park is situated in the Loess Hills and consists of bur oak-covered bluffs that rise steeply above the Big Sioux River Valley. Mount Talbot State Preserve just north of Stone State Park contains a 90-acre native prairie. The park contains a rich variety of birdlife, including nesting birds such as turkey vultures, barred owls, whip-poor-wills, wood thrushes, ovenbirds, Kentucky warblers, scarlet tanagers, and rufous-sided towhees. Wild turkeys, white-tailed deer, red foxes, raccoons, and opossums also live at this site.

Viewing Information: Stone State Park has more than 10 miles of hiking trails, including the self-guided Carolyn Benne Nature Trail. Wild turkeys and white-tailed deer are common and often seen from park roads. Gobbling turkeys can be heard in April and May. The spring wildflower bloom is excellent in May. Prairie areas contain a number of butterflies, including the rare Pawnee skipper, Olympia white, and Reakirt's blue. The small pond at the west end of Buzzard Roost Nature Trail has nesting wood ducks. Look for breeding Kentucky warblers and scarlet tanagers along the trail to the pond. On summer evenings, bats may be seen along park roads. Large numbers of raptors may be seen from September through October, including broad-winged and sharp-shinned hawks. In winter, check the feeders at the Regional Nature Center for fox squirrels, woodpeckers, black-capped chickadees, white-breasted nuthatches, northern cardinals, and American goldfinches.

Directions: *Stone State Park is on the east side of Iowa Highway 12 at the north edge of Sioux City. The new Regional Nature Center, headquarters of the Woodbury County Conservation Board, will open in September 1995, about 1 mile south of the park entrance along IA 12.*

Ownership: IDNR (712) 255-4698

Size: 1,085 acres

Closest Town: Sioux City

Iowa's native fauna included 140 species of fish, 68 mammals, 53 reptiles, and 23 amphibians. Due to the extensive loss of habitat in the state, many species have declined, and some, such as the bison, cougar, and skipjack herring, have been eliminated.

9. FIVE RIDGE PRAIRIE

Description: Nestled in the Loess Hills, this area offers a diversity of habitats, including bur oak forest and native prairie. There are great views of the surrounding Big Sioux River Valley. Wild turkeys and white-tailed deer are common. Nesting birds include yellow-billed cuckoos, great-crested flycatchers, eastern bluebirds, red-eyed vireos, rose-breasted grosbeaks, and indigo buntings. Several prairie butterflies, including the ottoe skipper and the regal fritillary, have been observed here. Some western species, such as the plains spadefoot toad and great plains toad, also have been seen here.

Viewing Information: This area is largely undeveloped, though its numerous fire breaks can serve as trails. A map displayed at the parking area shows the locations of the fire breaks. Generally, the western portions of the area are more scenic and contain more prairie. In spring, listen for displaying American woodcock in woodland openings. Along prairie edges, look for nesting field and lark sparrows. Bats are also common, especially near wooded ravines where they are seen at dusk throughout summer.

Directions: *From the north edge of Sioux City, follow Iowa Highway 12 north 6 miles and turn north on County Road K18. Proceed northeast 3.5 miles and turn west on 260th Street. Follow the road until it ends at a parking area.*

Ownership: Plymouth County Conservation Board (712) 947-4270; TNC (515) 244-5044

Size: 790 acres

Closest Town: Sioux City

Wildlife viewing generates $123 to $332 million in Iowa. To date there is no reliable funding to assist Iowa's 400-plus non-game wildlife species, or the nation's 1,800 non-game, non-endangered species. DON POGGENSEE

REGION TWO: PRAIRIE POTHOLE

The Prairie Pothole viewing region connects the topographical provinces of the Northwest Iowan Plains and the Des Moines Lobe. The northwest has the highest altitude in Iowa; consequently the area is drier, colder, and less forested than the rest of the state. The Des Moines Lobe represents Iowa's youngest landscape, which was caused by a glacial protrusion 14,000 years ago. The land is pocked with shallow depressions that hold thousands of prairie pothole wetlands. Major rivers were formed by swift-flowing glacial meltwater.

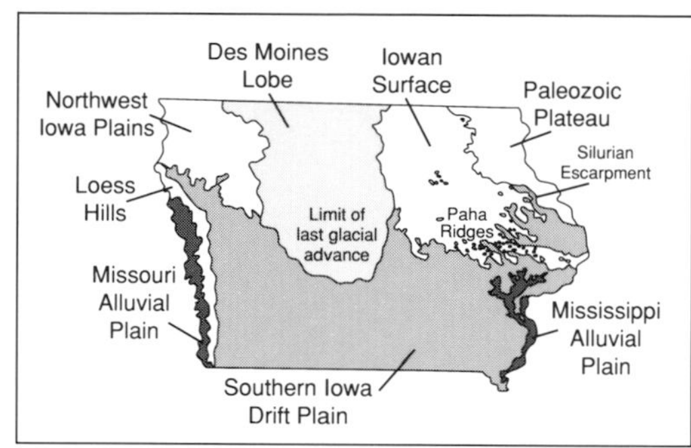

This area contains nearly all of Iowa's natural lakes. The lavish prairie wetlands once hosted nesting whooping and sandhill cranes, as well as hordes of waterfowl and shorebirds. Eventually, the water table dropped, drying even more wetlands. More than 95 percent of the area's wetlands have been drained, and the area's rich organic soils have been converted to some of the nation's finest farmland.

The wetlands and grassy uplands that remain provide nesting areas for mallards, Canada geese, American and least bitterns, black terns, yellow-headed blackbirds, and bobolinks. Blanding's turtles frequent these marshes, and chorus frogs sing from the grassy wetlands during warm periods from March through May. The region's woodlands follow the riverbeds and consist of oak-hickory on drier slopes and uplands; oak-maple-basswood on moist but well-drained uplands; and silver maple, ash, hackberry, black walnut, and cottonwood on the bottomlands. Wood ducks, barred owls, and eastern screech owls frequently nest in tree cavities in these areas.

Sites in this region vary from the prairie potholes of Spring Run Wildlife Area to the diverse plants of Kalsow Prairie, to the human-engineered Saylorville Reservoir—one of the best locations in the state to see American white pelicans and various gulls. Although native habitat loss has been tremendous, hundreds of wetlands have been recently restored by the North American Waterfowl Management Plan.

Prairie pothole marsh.
KEVIN MAGEE

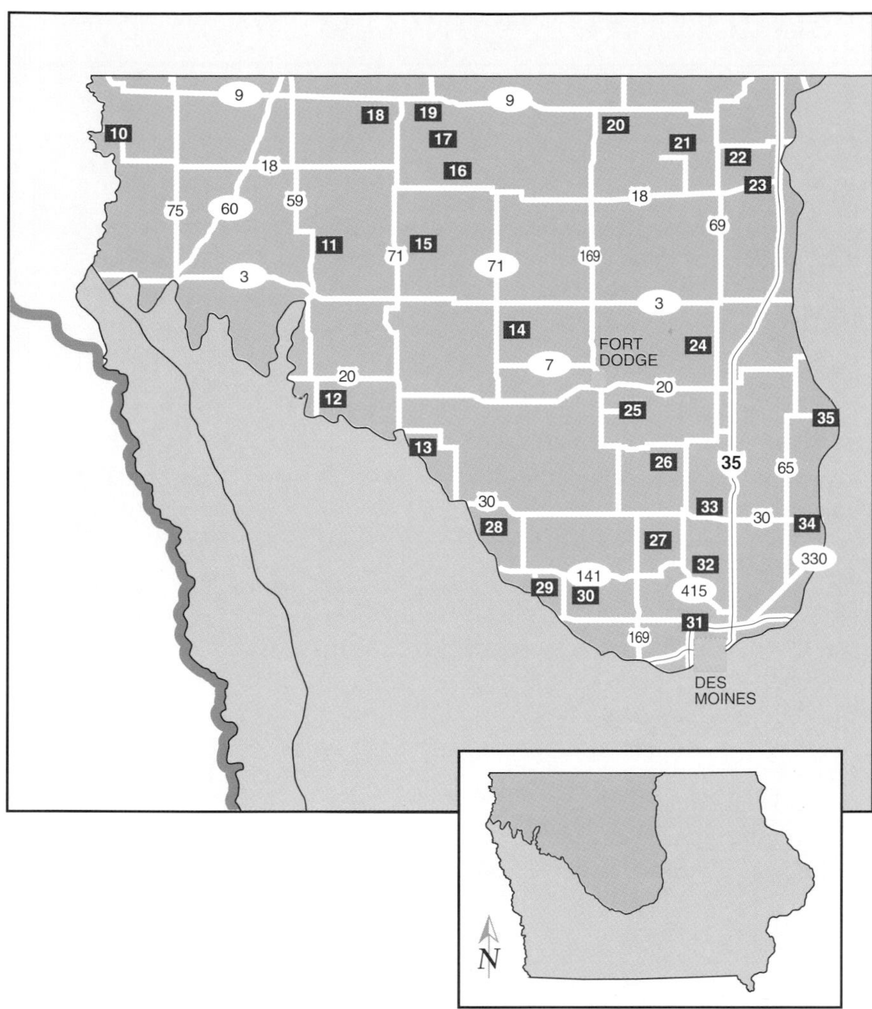

PRAIRIE POTHOLE

Wildlife Viewing Sites

10 Big Sioux Wildlife Area
11 Waterman Prairie Complex
12 Moorehead Park
13 Black Hawk State Park and Wildlife Area
14 Kalsow Prairie State Preserve
15 Kindlespire Little Sioux Access
16 Lost Island Nature Center
17 Spring Run Wildlife Area
18 Jemmerson Slough Wildlife Area
19 Spirit Lake Tour
20 Union Slough National Wildlife Refuge
21 Thorpe Park
22 Pilot Knob State Park
23 Clear Lake Tour
24 Big Wall Lake Wildlife Area
25 Dolliver Memorial State Park
26 Bjorkboda Marsh
27 Ledges State Park
28 Dunbar Slough Wildlife Area
29 Springbrook State Park
30 Bays Branch Wildlife Area
31 Saylorville Lake and Wildlife Area
32 Big Creek State Park and Wildlife Area
33 McFarland Park
34 Hendrickson Marsh Wildlife Area
35 Hardin County Greenbelt

PRAIRIE POTHOLES: AREAS WORTH RESTORING

Chorus frogs sing from the grass and sedge-meadow margins of wetlands while bitterns and yellow-headed blackbirds nest in cattails. Water lilies and arrowheads occupy deeper water. Tiny floating duckweed plants or submersed pondweed provide food for many species. Muskrat houses provide basking sites for Blanding's turtles or nest sites for Canada geese or black terns. Recently, hundreds of potholes have been restored by plugging old tile lines and allowing water to refill natural depressions.

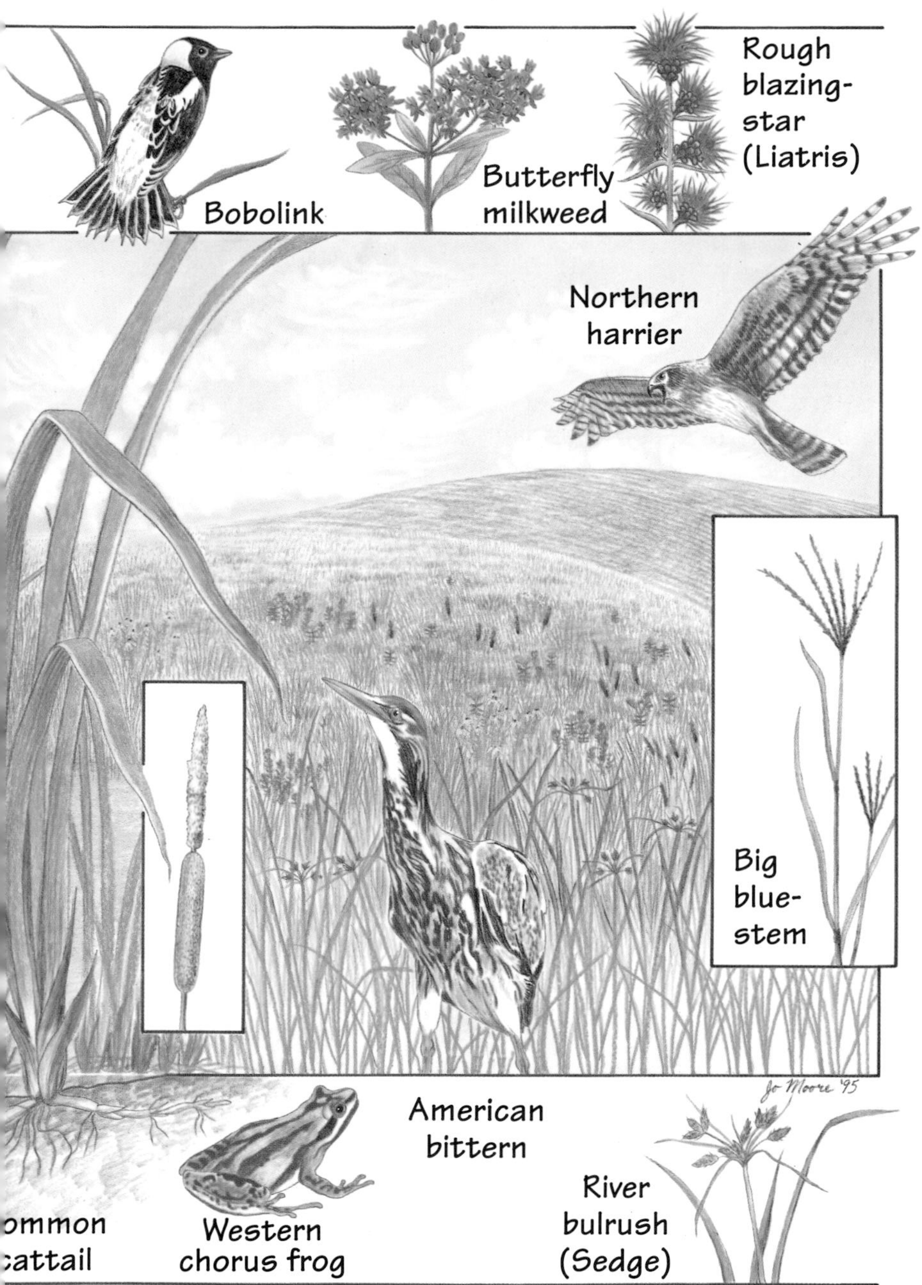

Large grassy uplands provide homes for bobolinks, dickcissels, upland sandpipers, northern harriers, and an array of grassland sparrows. Orange butterfly milkweed, purple coneflower, and gayfeather add color to tall or big bluestem, Indian grass and switchgrass stands. The somewhat shorter brome is a widely used non-native grass. Sites 16, 17, 19, and 20 provide excellent wetland tours while Sites 15, 22, 27, and 29 highlight the region's woodlands.

10. BIG SIOUX WILDLIFE AREA

Description: This rugged area borders the Big Sioux River. There are 3 parcels to explore, the Kroger Tract being the largest and most accessible. The area contains mostly mixed oak-cedar forest interspersed with open fields and prairie. White-tailed deer and wild turkeys are common residents. Red foxes and coyotes also are seen regularly. Nesting birds include red-tailed hawk, red-headed woodpecker, warbling vireo, rufous-sided towhee, and lark sparrow.

Viewing Information: There are no trails in the Big Sioux Wildlife Area, though numerous deer trails provide a good way to see it. Along the river, look for beavers, great blue herons, and bank and cliff swallows from spring through fall. In September and October, watch for migrant raptors from high points overlooking the river valley. Bald eagles are frequently seen during migration. *USE CAUTION DURING HUNTING SEASON.*

Directions: *To reach the Kroger Tract, take U.S. Highway 18 west of Inwood for 3 miles to Able Boulevard. There are several pullouts to the south on the west side of Able Blvd., and another parking area 0.8 mile west on the south side of US 18. The Nelson and Olson Tracts are located 2 and 4 miles north, respectively.*

Ownership: IDNR (712) 472-3751 **Size:** 758 acres

Closest Town: Inwood

11. WATERMAN PRAIRIE COMPLEX

Description: This recently acquired area contains a variety of habitats, including oak forest and restored prairie. The area harbors a large number of interesting mammals, including river otters, coyotes, and red foxes as well as white-tailed deer. The Little Sioux River bisects the area and is home to migrant and wintering bald eagles. Nesting birds include wild turkeys, eastern phoebes, wood thrushes, scarlet tanagers, rose-breasted grosbeaks, and field sparrows.

Viewing Information: The wooded areas of the Waterman Prairie Complex are home to wild turkeys, which are best seen in winter as they feed along edges of fields. Scan the river valley for bald eagles, and an occasional golden eagle, in winter. From the high bluffs, view migrating hawks from September through October. *USE CAUTION DURING HUNTING SEASON.*

Directions: *From the junction of Iowa Highway 10 and County Road M12 on the east edge of Sutherland, follow IA 10 south and east 5.2 miles and turn north on Yellow Avenue. Proceed 0.6 mile to a parking area, on the right, for Hannibal Waterman Wildlife Area. To reach Waterman Prairie Wildlife Area, return to IA 10. Proceed west 1.2 miles and turn north on Wilson Ave. Proceed 1.6 miles to a "T" intersection with Waterman Boulevard. Parking lots are 0.1 mile east and 1.2 miles west.*

Ownership: IDNR (712) 472-3751; O'Brien County Conservation Board (712) 448-2254

Size: 712 acres **Closest Town:** Sutherland

12. MOOREHEAD PARK

Description: This isolated woodland is an important bird sanctuary, with 182 species recorded. Summer residents include great-crested flycatchers, wood thrushes, Bell's and warbling vireos, bobolinks, and northern lined snakes. Watch for soaring turkey vultures and red-tailed hawks. Eastern bluebirds and American kestrels can be observed at nest boxes.

Viewing Information: Explore several miles of roads and hiking trails; a trail map is available at the park office. Observe 31 warbler species that migrate through here; peak time is about May 12. The oak savannah north of the old depot is a good area to see Blackburnian and other common warblers. Nesting Canada geese and wood ducks can be observed on the lake—also watch for beavers, mink, and great blue herons. During migration, bald eagles, ospreys, eared and horned grebes, and an occasional common loon may be seen. In winter, northern saw-whet owls are found in park pine plantings. *USE CAUTION DURING HUNTING SEASON.*

Directions: *From the junction of U.S. Highway 59 and Iowa Highway 175 west of Ida Grove, travel 0.6 mile east on IA 175 to the park entrance, on the north side of the road. Continue 0.4 mile northeast to the park office.*

Ownership: Ida County Conservation Board (712) 364-3300

Size: 258 acres

Closest Town: Ida Grove

13. BLACK HAWK STATE PARK AND WILDLIFE AREA

Description: Black Hawk Lake is the southernmost glacier-formed lake in Iowa. Nesting birds include wood ducks, great-crested flycatchers, warbling vireos, rose-breasted grosbeaks, and indigo buntings. Red foxes are occasionally seen; fox squirrels and raccoons are common.

Viewing Information: Black Hawk Lake and Inlet Marsh are good places for migrant waterfowl and American white pelicans, especially from March through April. Other water birds, including loons, ospreys, and terns are seen on the lake during migration. In March and November look for bald eagles perched in trees around the lake. The self-guided "Stubb" Severson Nature Trail offers viewing of migrant broad-winged hawks, flycatchers, thrushes, vireos, and warblers in May. Muskrats, green herons, belted kingfishers, and nesting Canada geese and wood ducks may be seen on Inlet Marsh in summer. *USE CAUTION IN SOME AREAS DURING HUNTING SEASON.*

Directions: *From U.S. Highway 71 in Lake View, turn south on Madison Street. Proceed 0.5 mile to 1st Street and turn east. Proceed 4 blocks to South Blossom Street and turn south. The park entrance is 2 blocks farther. Obtain park map at the park office on the left, just past the entrance.*

Ownership: IDNR (712) 657-8712 **Size:** 86 acres (957-acre lake)

Closest Town: Lake View

14. KALSOW PRAIRIE STATE PRESERVE

Description: This is one of Iowa's premier tallgrass prairies. Nesting birds include sedge wrens, common yellowthroats, dickcissels, grasshopper and swamp sparrows, bobolinks, and western meadowlarks. Upland sandpipers can be found here most years. Mammals include plains pocket gophers, red foxes, thirteen-lined ground squirrels, meadow jumping mice, and an occasional badger. Leopard and cricket frogs live in the potholes; smooth green snakes and northern prairie skinks have also been found here.

Viewing Information: There are no established paths in the Kalsow preserve, but the gentle terrain is easy to cover in a few hours. The list of wildlife found here is not long, but some species are common and allow close approach. By midsummer, as the prairie plants begin to flower, a variety of butterflies, ranging from the spectacular regal and great-spangled fritillaries to the inconspicuous wild indigo and two-spotted skipper, appear. *THIS IS A STATE PRESERVE; ALL PLANTS AND ANIMALS ARE PROTECTED.*

Directions: *From Iowa Highway 7 on the west edge of Manson, turn north on County Road N65 (Tabor Avenue). Proceed 4 miles and turn west on 630th Street. Proceed 1 mile to 280th Avenue. The prairie is on the left.*

Ownership: IDNR (712) 657-2639 or (515) 281-8676

Size: 160 acres

Closest Town: Manson

15. KINDLESPIRE LITTLE SIOUX ACCESS

Description: This tract of mature oak forest borders the Little Sioux River and is one of the most scenic woodlands in northwestern Iowa. White-tailed deer, wild turkeys, and red foxes are commonly seen. The area has a good diversity of birds, including migrant flycatchers, thrushes, warblers, and sparrows. Nesting birds include wood thrushes, yellow-throated and red-eyed vireos, ovenbirds, and scarlet tanagers, species that typically are found farther southeast.

Viewing Information: Best viewing is by hiking the trail south from the parking area along the creek. Branches of the trail lead to high, wooded ridges on either side of the valley and reconnect at the south end of the area. Wild turkeys may be seen anywhere in the area, as well as in fields west of the area entrance. A pair of scarlet tanagers summers along the creek south of the parking lot. Farther along the trail, look for nesting ovenbirds and red-eyed vireos. *USE CAUTION DURING HUNTING SEASON.*

Directions: *From Spencer, follow Iowa Highway 71 south 14.5 miles and turn east on 485th Street. Proceed 1.5 miles to 230th Avenue and continue east for 0.5 mile to a parking lot for the area.*

Ownership: Clay County Conservation Board (712) 262-2187

Size: 222 acres

Closest Town: Sioux Rapids

16. LOST ISLAND NATURE CENTER

Description: The Lost Island Nature Center and nearby wetlands trail provide an excellent introduction to the prairie pothole habitat that once covered much of northern Iowa. Nesting birds include pied-billed grebes, American and least bitterns, Canada geese, blue-winged teal, Virginia rails, soras, willow flycatchers, marsh wrens, swamp sparrows, bobolinks, and yellow-headed blackbirds. The area teems with migrant ducks and geese in spring. Deer, red foxes, striped skunks, and raccoons are common; badgers are seen occasionally. Several species of frogs, tiger salamanders, and painted, snapping, and Blanding's turtles occupy the ponds.

Viewing Information: The Nature Trail follows a series of old dikes and offers good viewing of many wetland species at close range. Migrant waterfowl are abundant from March through April. From May through July most of the above species can be seen in the marshes. American white pelicans are present from April to September. Painted and snapping turtles are often seen in May and June, when they lay their eggs along roadsides. Nearby 960-acre Deweys Pasture Wildlife Area is a prime example of prairie pothole habitat and is best seen on foot. Look for migrant waterfowl and nesting marsh birds.

Directions: *From the junction of U.S. Highway 18 and County Road N18 west of Ruthven, follow CR N18 (340th Avenue) north 3.6 miles and turn east on 320th Street. Proceed east along Lost Island Lake 1.8 miles to the nature center entrance, on the right (call for hours). To reach Deweys Pasture, return to CR N18 and turn north. Proceed 1 mile to the area on the right.*

Ownership: Palo Alto County Conservation Board (712) 837-4866; IDNR (712) 262-4177

Size: 129 acres **Closest Town:** Ruthven

Native praries such as Kalsow (see opposite page) may contain more than 250 types of plants and 3,000 types of insects. Seventy species of butterflies use Iowa prairies.
CARL KURTZ

17. SPRING RUN WILDLIFE AREA

Description: Spring Run is one of the best examples of the prairie pothole habitat that once covered much of Iowa. The area is dotted with dozens of small marshes that attract both grassland and wetland species. Nesting birds include American bitterns, Canada geese, blue-winged teal, redheads, Virginia rails, soras, American coots, willow flycatchers, dickcissels, and savannah sparrows. Mammals include muskrats, red foxes, badgers, plains pocket gophers, and white-tailed deer. Cricket and chorus frogs are common.

Viewing Information: The best way to see this area is by foot. Thousands of migrant waterfowl, especially Canada geese and dabbling ducks, stop here in March and April. In May, flocks of American golden-plovers and other shorebirds use the area. Nesting marsh birds are best seen May through June. Many Franklin's and ring-billed gulls and black and Forster's terns often stop here. In May and from July through August, lesser yellowlegs, and least and pectoral sandpipers use the area. *USE CAUTION DURING HUNTING SEASON.*

Directions: *From the junction of Iowa Highway 9 and Iowa Highway 276 in Spirit Lake, follow IA 9 east 0.7 mile and turn south on County Road M56 (260th Avenue). Proceed 4.7 miles and turn east on 190th Street. Proceed 2 miles and turn north on 280th Avenue. Continue for 0.5 mile and turn west on a road that goes diagonally through the center of the area. Public lands extend 2 miles south and 4 miles west.*

Ownership: IDNR (712) 472-3751; USFWS

Size: 2,605 acres **Closest Town:** Spirit Lake

18. JEMMERSON SLOUGH WILDLIFE AREA

Description: A premier marsh, home to about 20 species of nesting wetland birds, including pied-billed grebes, Virginia rails, soras, American coots, black terns, willow flycatchers, marsh wrens, swamp sparrows, and yellow-headed blackbirds. Black-crowned night-herons and Forster's terns nest here occasionally.White-tailed deer, raccoons, muskrats, and mink are resident. Leopard frogs, bullfrogs, and painted turtles are common.

Viewing Information: The parking area on the south side is the best vantage point. During migration, waterfowl, American white pelicans, and double-crested cormorants often stop here. A few pelicans often spend the summer. The bur oak stand around the parking area is good for migrant warblers, vireos, flycatchers, and other woodland species. This is an excellent marsh to explore by canoe. Good views of the marsh can also be obtained from 140th Street. *USE CAUTION DURING HUNTING SEASON.*

Directions: *From the junction of Iowa Highways 9 and 276 in Spirit Lake, follow IA 9 west 2.1 miles and turn east on 153rd Street. Proceed 0.5 mile and turn north onto a narrow gravel road that leads to the south side of the marsh.*

Ownership: IDNR (712) 472-3751; USFWS

Size: 855 acres **Closest Town:** Spirit Lake

19. SPIRIT LAKE TOUR

Description: This tour highlights some of the areas to view wildlife in the Spirit Lake region. Migrant loons, grebes, American white pelicans, waterfowl, Franklin's gulls, and terns are observed here regularly. Nesting birds include pied-billed grebes, least bitterns, Canada geese, redheads, ruddy ducks, Virginia rails, Forster's and black terns, marsh wrens, and yellow-headed blackbirds. White-tailed deer, muskrats, raccoons, mink, red foxes, and gray partridges reside here.

Viewing Information: Orleans Beach offers views of the south end of Spirit Lake. Look for migrant waterfowl, loons, and other water birds. At Hales Slough, look for American white pelicans during migration and in summer. At Trickle Slough, scan the north side of Spirit Lake for migrant waterfowl, loons, and grebes. Mini-Wakan State Park is good for migrant warblers and other passerines in May and September. Scan the rock jetty west of the boat ramp for Franklin's gulls and Forster's terns in summer. Marble Beach State Park overlooks the west side of Spirit Lake. Scan the lake for waterfowl, loons, and terns in migration. The pen at the north end of the Kettleson Waterfowl Production Area has several pairs of trumpeter swans as part of the reintroduction program. In late summer, look for shorebirds, Franklin's gulls, and Forster's terns on the island here. From the boat ramp west of the Big Sioux Wildlife Unit headquarters at Kettleson Hogsback, scan the south end of Hottes Lake for nesting redheads and ruddy ducks. American white pelicans are here from April to September. McBreen Marsh has nesting American and least bitterns, Virginia rails, and yellow-headed blackbirds. From the boat ramp at the southwest end of Grover's Lake, look for migrant waterfowl from March through April and nesting black-crowned night-herons, American coots, and Forster's and black terns in summer. *USE CAUTION IN SOME AREAS DURING HUNTING SEASON.*

Directions: *See map at right. Begin at the Spirit Lake Fish Hatchery. From the junction of Iowa Highways 9 and 276 in Spirit Lake, follow IA 276 north 1.5 mile to a "T" intersection and turn east on Iowa Highway 327. Proceed 0.3 mile and turn south on 252nd Avenue. The hatchery is on the right. Maps of the area are available here.*

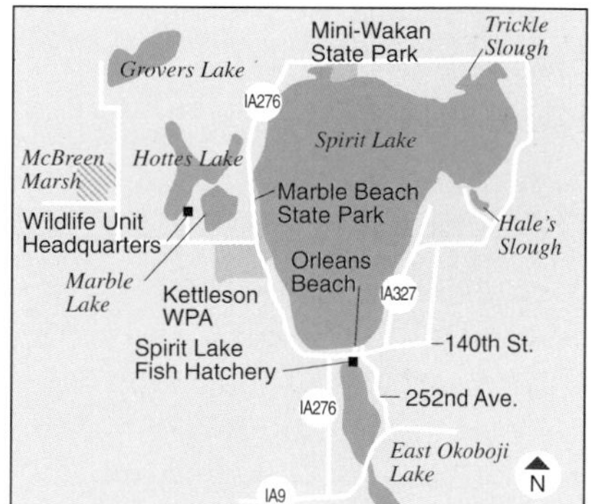

Ownership: IDNR (712) 472-3751; USFWS

Size: 8,000 acres

Closest Town: Spirit Lake

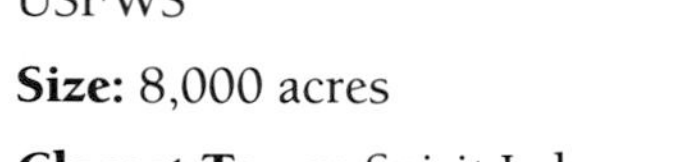

PRAIRIE POTHOLE

20. UNION SLOUGH NATIONAL WILDLIFE REFUGE

Description: Union Slough is a haven for migratory and nesting waterfowl and migrant shorebirds. The refuge includes 1,300 acres of open water and marsh, with the remaining area comprising a variety of upland habitats, mostly grasslands. Pied-billed grebes, least bitterns, hooded mergansers, Virginia rails, gray partridges, swamp sparrows, bobolinks, and yellow-headed blackbirds all nest on the refuge. White-tailed deer, red foxes, mink, muskrats, raccoons, and striped skunks are residents. Painted and snapping turtles are common in summer.

Viewing Information: Access to the refuge is limited to roadside viewing, except for several short trails and a self-guided auto tour, open in September and October (check with the refuge for specific dates). The best time to visit the area is from March to May. During March and April, thousands of waterfowl can be seen, mostly dabbling ducks such as mallards, blue- and green-winged teal, gadwalls, and American wigeon. Canada and snow geese occur in large numbers, and a few tundra swans stop each spring. Up to 20 species of waterfowl can be seen on a spring day. Mallards, blue-winged teal, and wood ducks are common breeders. Other common migrants include American white pelicans, great egrets, bald eagles, Franklin's gulls, Forster's terns, and a variety of warblers and other passerines. During summer and fall, one or more of the main pools may be drawn down, attracting thousands of shorebirds and herons. In winter, hundreds of ring-necked pheasants may be seen in fields around the refuge, especially if there is snow cover.

Directions: *From the junction of U.S. Highway 169 and County Road A42 on the south side of Bancroft, follow CR A42 east 6.8 miles to the refuge headquarters, on the right. A refuge map and brochure are available during regular business hours (Monday through Friday, 7:30 a.m. - 4 p.m.).*

Ownership: USFWS (515) 928-2523

Size: 2,845 acres

Closest Town: Bancroft

Blue-winged teal are the most common breeding ducks in Iowa's pothole region. Like most dabbling ducks, teal nest in grasslands near water. After the eggs hatch, they move their brood to water.

TY SMEDES

21. THORPE PARK

Description: This park is home to a pair of trumpeter swans, part of Iowa's recent reintroduction program. Migrant waterfowl are abundant. White-tailed deer, red foxes, mink, and a few wild turkeys are resident. Nesting birds include Canada geese, wood ducks, willow flycatchers, sedge and marsh wrens, and yellow warblers. Leopard and cricket frogs live in the wetlands.

Viewing Information: Much of this viewing area is visible from a car, and several miles of trails provide excellent access. Waterfowl are easily observed on Lake Catherine and in marshes at adjacent Russ Wildlife Area in March and April. Trumpeter swans and a few Canada geese are year-round residents on Lake Catherine. Nesting marsh birds are best observed at Russ Wildlife Area. *USE CAUTION DURING HUNTING SEASON.*

Directions*: From the junction of U.S. Highway 69 and County Road B14 in Forest City, follow CR B14 west for 5.3 miles and turn north on Maple Avenue (which becomes 120th Avenue in Winnebago County). Proceed 1.5 miles and turn west on 345th Street. Proceed 1 mile to the park entrance on the left.*

Ownership: Winnebago County Conservation Board (515) 565-3390;

Size: 160 acres

Closest Town: Forest City

22. PILOT KNOB STATE PARK

Description: At an elevation of 1,450 feet, Pilot Knob is the second highest point in Iowa and provides scenic views of the Winnebago River and surrounding lands. The park also includes Dead Man's Lake, the only floating sphagnum bog in Iowa. White-tailed deer, wild turkeys, and red foxes are residents. Nesting birds include green herons, wood thrushes, red-eyed vireos, scarlet tanagers, and northern orioles. The park and surrounding lands are the only places in Iowa where Gapper's red-backed voles can be found.

Viewing Information: Park roads and 13.5 miles of trails provide good access to the park's habitats. White-tailed deer and wild turkeys are common throughout the park and easily seen in winter. Ruffed grouse are occasionally seen. From the observation tower, view the surrounding landscape for a distance of at least 30 miles.

Directions: *From the junction of Iowa Highway 9 and U.S. Highway 69 in Forest City, follow IA 9 east for 3.3 miles and turn south on 205th Avenue. Proceed 1 mile to the park entrance. Park maps are available at the park office.*

Ownership: IDNR (515) 581-4835

Size: 700 acres

Closest Town: Forest City

23. CLEAR LAKE TOUR

Description: This tour highlights several wildlife areas around Clear Lake. Migrant grebes, American white pelicans, waterfowl, rails, shorebirds, gulls, and terns commonly are seen. Mammals that live in the Clear Lake area include muskrats, mink, ermine, white-tailed deer, red foxes, and raccoons. Nesting birds include pied-billed grebes, Canada geese, blue-winged teal, Virginia rails, black terns, willow flycatchers, tree swallows, and yellow-headed blackbirds. Cricket, chorus, and leopard frogs, American toads, and tiger salamanders are residents.

Viewing Information: Begin at the fisheries and wildlife station, where maps of the area are available. Scan Clear Lake for migrant loons, grebes, waterfowl, Franklin's gulls, and terns. Aerators east of McIntosh Woods State Park are excellent places to see migrant waterfowl in March before the lake thaws, with a few mallards and Canada geese sometimes wintering there. McIntosh Wildlife Area is a good place to see migrant waterfowl, herons, rails, and shorebirds from March through May, with some waterfowl remaining to nest. McIntosh Woods State Park is excellent for seeing migrant warblers, thrushes, and other passerines in May and September. White-tailed deer are often seen in the park. The beach may harbor migrant shorebirds, gulls, and terns. Ventura Marsh, visible from the boat ramp at the east end off County Road S14 or from parking lots on old U.S. Highway 18, is excellent for migrant waterfowl in March and April. A canoe is a great way to see the marsh. Expect nesting least bitterns, wood ducks, Virginia rails, Forster's and black terns, marsh wrens, and yellow-headed blackbirds, plus numerous muskrats and perhaps a mink. The marsh is good for American white pelicans in April and September. Ventura Marsh is also the site of a trumpeter swan reintroduction. The swan pens are located on the south side of the marsh, 0.5 mile west of CR S14. Lekwa Marsh is excellent for migrant waterfowl in March and April and has nesting yellow-headed blackbirds. The total tour route encompasses 12 to 25 miles of driving. *USE CAUTION IN SOME AREAS DURING HUNTING SEASONS.*

Directions: *See map below. From Interstate 35, take the Clear Lake/U.S. Highway 18 exit (Exit 194). Follow US 18 west 2.7 miles and turn south on 16th Street West. Proceed 1 block to a "T" intersection and turn east on West 7th Avenue North. Continue to a "Y" with North Shore Drive. The fisheries and wildlife station is on the south side of this intersection.*

Ownership: IDNR (515) 357-3517 **Size:** 4,690 acres

Closest Town: Clear Lake

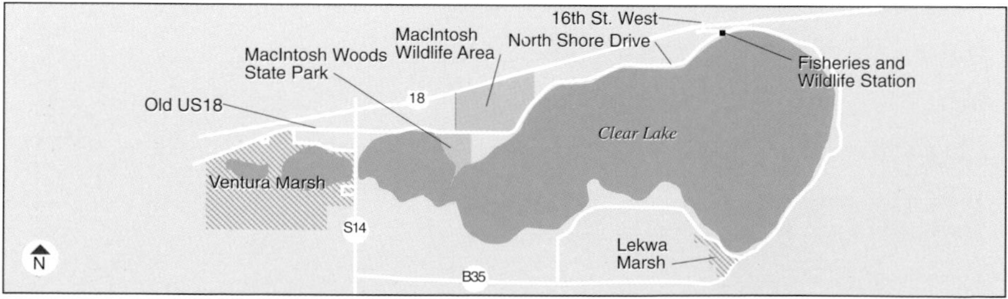

IOWA THEN AND NOW

Prior to 1830

Numerous elk, bison, whooping cranes, sandhill cranes, ducks, shorebirds and prairie chickens used Iowa's vast prairies and wetlands. Woodlands harbored black bears and cougars.

1850-1930

The expansive prairies were plowed under; 95 percent of the state was converted to farmland. Many species disappeared, although prairie chickens thrived briefly, then vanished in the 1950s.

The Present

Pioneer-planted trees matured, farm size increased, and crop diversity decreased. Cooperative programs helped restore wetlands, acquire land, reintroduce native wildlife, and manage for wildlife diversity.

24. BIG WALL LAKE WILDLIFE AREA

Description: This shallow, natural marsh is one of the largest remaining in Iowa. The area is a haven for aquatic birds, especially waterfowl. Nesting birds include pied-billed grebes, American and least bitterns, blue-winged teal, Virginia rails, common moorhens, black terns, marsh wrens, swamp sparrows, and yellow-headed blackbirds. Muskrats are abundant, and mink are frequently seen along the marsh edge. Painted and snapping turtles and leopard frogs are common during the warmer months.

Viewing Information: Much of the wildlife can be viewed from the main boat ramp or at ramps a mile to the north on the east side, and at the northwest end. However, the best way to see the area is by canoe. During March and April, the marsh often contains thousands of waterfowl, dominated by puddle ducks like mallards, blue- and green-winged teal, gadwalls, and northern shovelers. Large numbers of ring-necked and ruddy ducks have also been seen here. In April, watch for tiger salamanders on roads surrounding the marsh. In summer, snapping and painted turtles bask on muskrat huts. Thousands of yellow-headed blackbirds nest and are easily approached by canoe. Migrant shorebirds are sometimes common when water levels are low. From late June through July, scan the marsh at dusk for duck broods and least bitterns. *USE CAUTION DURING HUNTING SEASON.*

Directions: *From the junction of U.S. Highway 69 and Iowa Highway 928 in Blairsburg, follow US 69 north 10 miles and turn west on a gravel road. Proceed west 0.5 mile to the main boat ramp overlooking the marsh.*

Ownership: IDNR (515) 456-3730

Size: 978 acres

Closest Town: Clarion

Muskrats are the most conspicuous mammals of Iowa's prairie wetlands. Their mounds also provide nest sites for ducks, Canada geese, and black terns. TY SMEDES

25. DOLLIVER MEMORIAL STATE PARK

Description: Located along the Des Moines River Valley, this area includes mature oak-hickory and bottomland forest. Nesting birds include barred owls, ruby-throated hummingbirds, Acadian flycatchers, yellow-throated vireos, cerulean warblers, American redstarts, ovenbirds, and scarlet tanagers. White-tailed deer, red foxes, and wild turkeys are residents.

Viewing Information: The trail through the southeast corner of the park offers scenic views of the river valley. Forest openings along the river are good spots to view migrant hawks from September through October. Many breeding birds can be seen from the road along Prairie Creek between the Group Camp area and the campground. White-tailed deer are commonly seen here as well. The trail west along Prairie Creek from the Group Camp area is especially worth walking. It offers good opportunities to see many woodland bird species, especially scarlet tanager, and provides scenic views of the park. Bats, including little brown myotis, are common in summer.

Directions: *From Lehigh, follow Iowa Highway 50 west for 1 mile and turn north on a paved road. Proceed north 0.6 mile to the park entrance.*

Ownership: IDNR (515) 359-2539

Size: 600 acres

Closest Town: Lehigh

26. BJORKBODA MARSH

Description: This natural marsh is a good place to observe more than 85 marsh and grassland nesting birds, and listen to the spring courtship songs of 5 frog species and the American toad. Summer residents include Canada geese, yellow-headed blackbirds, killdeer, sedge and marsh wrens, soras, and painted turtles. Great blue herons and great egrets are common. View numerous species of waterfowl during migration. Greater and lesser yellowlegs and black terns also frequent the marsh during migration.

Viewing Information: Best viewing of migrating shorebirds is from April through May and from August through September; for waterfowl, best times are March and April and from September through November—for best viewing, stay in your vehicle and use a spotting scope. Good viewing of migrating raptors over adjacent grasslands April through May and September through October. Large flocks of ring-necked pheasants can be observed during winter months north of the marsh.

Directions: *From Stanhope, travel south on Iowa Highway 17 for 4 miles and turn west on the gravel road marked by a sign. Proceed west 1 mile, then 1 mile south to an intersection. From there, go 0.1 mile west and into the signed parking lot on the north side of the road.*

Ownership: Hamilton County Conservation Board (515) 832-9570

Size: 36 acres

Closest Town: Stanhope

27. LEDGES STATE PARK

Description: Located along the scenic Des Moines River Valley, the park offers a variety of habitats including a mature oak forest, old fields, and a restored prairie. More than 200 species of birds have been recorded in the park, including nesting birds such as broad-winged hawks, veeries, northern parulas, yellow-throated, cerulean, and Kentucky warblers, Louisiana waterthrushes, and scarlet tanagers. Wild turkeys and white-tailed deer are common residents. The park also harbors several bat species, including Keen's myotis and red and hoary bats.

Viewing Information: The restored prairie near the campground has nesting eastern and western meadowlarks and is a good place to see displaying American woodcocks in March and April. In upland forest along the first part of the loop drive are nesting ovenbirds, red-eyed vireos, and scarlet tanagers, plus several mammals, including eastern chipmunks. In the scenic lower canyon, listen for wild turkeys gobbling in April and May and watch for bats in summer. At the junction of Pease and Davis creeks, look for cerulean warblers and Louisiana waterthrushes in summer. The migration of flycatchers, warblers, vireos, thrushes, and other passerines can be excellent in the lower canyon in May and September. Along the Des Moines River, watch for turkey vultures and belted kingfishers in summer and migrant bald eagles from November through December. The Lost Lake Nature Trail is good for nesting wood thrushes and blue-winged warblers. A scenic overlook west of Lost Lake offers views of the river valley and is good for viewing migrant hawks from September through October.

Directions: *From the junction of U.S. Highway 30 and Iowa Highway 17 east of Boone, follow IA 17 south 2.6 miles and turn west on 250th Street. Proceed west 3 miles and turn south on P Avenue. Proceed 0.2 mile to the park office, on the right, where a park map can be obtained.*

Ownership: IDNR (515) 432-1852

Size: 1,200 acres

Closest Town: Boone

Bobolinks may migrate 5,000 miles or more to South America each winter. Although still observed statewide, bobolink populations have significantly declined because of the loss of large, undisturbed grasslands. The distinctive notes of their song give them their name. DON POGGENSEE

28. DUNBAR SLOUGH WILDLIFE AREA

Description: This reconstructed prairie marsh is an excellent area for viewing a large variety of waterfowl and other wetland-associated species. Canada geese, mallards, wood ducks, and American coots are common as are ring-necked pheasants, white-tailed deer, raccoons, and cottontail rabbits. Research has found nesting evidence for 77 species, including loggerhead shrikes, yellow-headed blackbirds, marsh wrens, swamp sparrows, and great-tailed grackles. Listen for American toads, chorus, cricket, leopard, and gray tree frog songs from April through July. Be watchful for swimming muskrats and meandering mink. The north pool is a good place to view summering American white pelicans and great blue herons. Red-tailed hawks and American kestrels nest nearby. Northern harriers are often seen during October, and bald eagles and ospreys are sometimes seen during migration.

Viewing Information: During spring migration, large numbers of many waterfowl species can be viewed including mallards, lesser scaup, ring-necked ducks, and buffleheads. The south-central parking lot, which also contains an undeveloped boat ramp, is particularly good for viewing. During summer months, viewing from a canoe can be very rewarding. At the south end of the marsh is a newly constructed 60-acre wetland, which is visible from the road and should provide good viewing of shorebirds. A boardwalk, barrier-free trails, and an interpretive/education center planned for this area. *PLEASE VIEW WILDLIFE FROM YOUR VEHICLE AT THE INVIOLATE WATERFOWL REFUGE FROM SEPTEMBER 15 THROUGH DECEMBER 25. PUBLIC HUNTING OCCURS ON MANY AREAS; PLEASE USE CAUTION.*

Directions: *From the intersection of U.S. Highway 30 and County Road N58 north of Ralston, drive south on CR N58 for 6 miles; turn left on a gravel road and proceed 0.2 mile to parking lot on north side of road. Boat access is 0.8 mile farther east and 0.5 mile north.*

Ownership: IDNR (515) 993-3911; Education Center to be managed by the Greene County Conservation Board (515) 386-4629

Size: 1,369 acres

Closest Towns: Ralston, Scranton

Iowa's state bird, the American goldfinch, is the last bird to nest in the year. It prefers to wait until August and September when ripe milkweeds, cattails, goldenrods, and asters are available for constructing its nest and feeding its young.

29. SPRINGBROOK STATE PARK

Description: This park is comprised mostly of oak-hickory forest and is situated in the Raccoon River Valley. The park is also the site of the Conservation Education Center and a 15-acre manmade lake. The park is best known for the large white-tailed deer herd that resides here. Wild turkeys, red and gray foxes, coyotes, raccoons, and beavers are residents. Nesting birds include wood ducks, barred owls, red-headed woodpeckers, eastern phoebes, tufted titmice, red-eyed vireos, scarlet tanagers, and rose-breasted grosbeaks.

Viewing Information: The park is accessible from several roads and more than 5 miles of trails. White-tailed deer are abundant in the park and are easily seen year-round, particularly at dusk. Wild turkeys also are common and can be heard gobbling in April and May. Along the Raccoon River, look for beavers, migrant great blue herons, and nesting wood ducks and belted kingfishers. The Conservation Education Center (open Monday through Friday, 8 a.m. - 4:30 p.m.) has exhibits of local fauna. There is also a self-guided nature trail north of the center. Check the bird feeders here for common winter species, including woodpeckers and American goldfinches.

Directions: *From the junction of Iowa Highways 25 and 44 in Guthrie Center, proceed north on IA 25 for 7.3 miles and turn east on Iowa Highway 384. Proceed east 1.2 miles to the park entrance. Proceed east another 0.4 mile to the park office, on the left.*

Ownership: IDNR (515) 747-3591

Size: 786 acres

Closest town: Yale

Wildlife viewing often requires good judgment. Never approach nesting birds in the spring. If you happen upon a nest with eggs, such as this wild turkey nest, leave immediately, since turkeys and other birds will abandon their eggs if they are harassed or approached too closely. TODD FINK

30. BAYS BRANCH WILDLIFE AREA

Description: Located near the Raccoon River valley, this area has a variety of habitats, including a shallow lake, grasslands, and planted hedgerows. The area is known for fall concentrations of Canada geese, mallards, and other waterfowl. Several trumpeter swans reside in the goose pen as part of a reintroduction program. Red foxes, white-tailed deer, coyotes, muskrats, and river otters are residents. Nesting birds include Canada geese, killdeer, yellow warblers, and orchard orioles.

Viewing Information: View migrant and wintering waterfowl from the overlook at the south end of the lake or from the road along the goose pen. March has the greatest diversity, though the peak of 20,000 geese and 15,000 ducks is usually in November. Puddle ducks are numerous, along with canvasbacks, ring-necked ducks, and lesser scaup. In March and November, scan the goose flocks for a greater white-fronted or Ross's goose. The south end of the lake is a waterfowl refuge from September 15 through December 25, and trespassing is not permitted during this time. Bald eagles and ospreys may pass through here during migration. Shorebird numbers peak in May and August when water levels are low. Flocks of American white pelicans frequently can be seen here in April and September. Along the west side of the lake, about 1.5 miles north of the goose pen, are several scattered stands of red cedar and plantings of pine that may harbor wintering long-eared and short-eared owls. White-tailed deer are common in the brushy and wooded edges along the lake. River otters have been seen on the lake occasionally. *USE CAUTION DURING HUNTING SEASON.*

Directions: *From the junction of Iowa Highways 4 and 44 in Panora, follow IA 4 north 1.8 miles and turn east on 200th Street. Proceed east 1.6 miles to the area on the left. From here, drive north along the west side of the goose pen or continue east another 0.3 mile to a pullout on the left that overlooks the area.*

Ownership: IDNR (515) 993-3911

Size: 842 acres

Closest Town: Panora

During winter, Iowa attracts some of the largest concentrations of bald eagles in the lower 48 states. The eagles are particularly attracted to dams because the turbulent water below the dam is free of ice, allowing the eagles to procure their major food—fish.

31. SAYLORVILLE LAKE AND WILDLIFE AREA

Description: Located in the Des Moines River Valley, this area is known for its diversity of birdlife, with more than 300 species observed here. Large numbers of loons, grebes, American white pelicans, waterfowl, bald eagles, shorebirds, and gulls frequent the lake during migration. The wooded bluffs surrounding the lake attract migrant songbirds and nesting Cooper's hawks, wild turkeys, barred owls, Acadian flycatchers, cerulean warblers, American redstarts, and ovenbirds. White-tailed deer are abundant, with coyotes, red and gray foxes, and several species of bats also present.

Viewing Information: The visitor center offers interpretive materials, wildlife displays and nature programs (call for details). In winter, check the bird feeders for fox squirrels and residents, such as red-bellied woodpeckers and tufted titmice, plus an occasional purple finch. Just north of the visitor center is a butterfly garden, which may have swallowtails and ruby-throated hummingbirds. The pullouts on the dam are excellent vantage points to view migrant loons, grebes, waterfowl, and gulls from March through April and October through November. Bald eagles roost in trees along the west shore of the lake above Lakeview, and gather on the ice above the dam in March. Concentrations of 75 or more have been present. Watch for coyotes and red foxes on the ice here in winter. An observation deck at Lakeview overlooks a small pond and marsh. Beavers, wood ducks, and great blue herons are present from spring through fall. In early October, large numbers of wood ducks often gather here at dusk. Scan the far hillside for wild turkeys in winter. The north end of the lake, viewed from the shoulder of Iowa Highway 17 or Lewis A. Jester County Park, is home to double-crested cormorants, shorebirds, and several species of herons during migration. Thousands of American white pelicans may gather here in September. *USE CAUTION IN SOME AREAS DURING HUNTING SEASON.*

Directions: *From Interstate 35 north of Des Moines, take the Ankeny/Iowa Highway 160 exit (Exit 90). Follow IA 160 west for 2.3 miles where it becomes Iowa Highway 415. Continue west another 2.6 miles and turn west on N.W. 84th Avenue. Follow signs to the visitor center for a map of the area.*

Ownership: USACOE (515) 276-4656; IDNR (515) 432-2235

Size: 26,000 acres

Closest Town: Johnston

From March through May, the diminutive chorus frog sings from grassy wetlands and ditches; its song is similar to the sound produced by running your finger across the teeth of a comb. CARL KURTZ

32. BIG CREEK STATE PARK AND WILDLIFE AREA

Description: This large lake and surrounding upland are adjacent to the Des Moines River Valley. The lake attracts migrant loons, grebes, American white pelicans, waterfowl, gulls, and terns. The lake is surrounded by a variety of habitats including mixed oak-cedar forest, grassy fields, and planted hedgerows. White-tailed deer are common residents, with red foxes and coyotes also present. Nesting birds include willow flycatchers, Bell's vireos, yellow warblers, indigo buntings, and eastern and western meadowlarks.

Viewing Information: Migrant water birds are best viewed from March through May and from September through November from the pullout near the jetty east of 100th Street and from the boat ramp north of the beach. Thousands of mallards and Canada geese often gather on the lake in November and December, along with common goldeneyes, buffleheads, and numerous other ducks. In summer, expect lots of boats on the lake as well as nesting Canada geese. Look for willow flycatchers and Bell's vireos along the road between the beach and fishing pier on the east side of the lake. The area is good for winter raptors, including northern harrier and red-tailed and rough-legged hawks. Long-eared and northern saw-whet owls are regular winter visitors in cedar groves along the west side of the lake. In winter, white-tailed deer are easily seen along the road on the east side of the park. *USE CAUTION DURING HUNTING SEASON, OUTSIDE OF THE STATE PARK.*

***Directions:** From Polk City, follow Iowa Highway 415 (also N.W. Madrid Drive) northwest 1.9 miles and turn west on N.W. 125th Avenue. Proceed 0.4 mile to park office on your left. Obtain a map of the area here.*

Ownership: IDNR (515) 984-6473, (515) 432-2235

Size: 3,550 acres

Closest Town: Polk City

Neotropical migrants include songbirds such as warblers, vireos, and flycatchers. These birds breed in North America and winter from the Gulf Coast to South America. Of the 110 Midwestern migrants, 39 face extirpation or severe threats from habitat loss, disturbance, predation, chemicals, and low nesting success.

33. MCFARLAND PARK

Description: A good blend of tallgrass prairie, woodland, and streamside habitats makes this area attractive to a wide variety of wildlife. At least 70 species of birds nest nearby. Watch and listen for bobolinks, meadowlarks, sedge wrens, and dickcissels in the prairie; great-crested flycatchers, barred owls, and red-bellied woodpeckers in the woods; and indigo buntings, northern orioles, ring-necked pheasants, and red-tailed hawks at the woodland edge. During spring months at the lake and streams listen for the songs of eastern and Cope's gray tree frogs, chorus and leopard frogs, and American toads. Ospreys, and pied-billed grebes frequent the lake during migration, and wood ducks as well as painted and snapping turtles can be seen on the lake when it is not frozen. Woodland wildflowers are best seen in April and May and prairie flowers from May through August.

Viewing Information: The Story County Conservation Center is the park's headquarters for environmental education. A year-round bird-feeding station at the center draws such birds as blue jays, northern cardinals, American goldfinches, pine siskins, house finches, and downy woodpeckers. An extensive 5.5-mile trail system includes the hard-surfaced Touch-a-Life Trail, which meanders around a 6.5-acre lake and through meadows and woods. Maps are available at the center. Watch for eastern bluebirds, black-capped chickadees, and house wrens using nest boxes along the trail, and be on the lookout at dusk and dawn for white-tailed deer, raccoons, or opossums and perhaps even a coyote, red fox, or wild turkey. A butterfly garden directly north of the center is a great place to observe butterflies during summer months. The best times for viewing wildlife are weekdays. Contact the Story County Conservation Center for scheduled programs, workshops, and field trips.

Directions: *From Interstate 35 north of Ames, take Exit 116. Go west 0.6 mile on County Road E29. Turn north at stop sign onto Dayton Road and travel 1 mile. At the "T" intersection go east 0.5 mile to the Story County Conservation Center parking lot, on the north side of the road.*

Ownership: Story County Conservation Board (515) 232-2516

Size: 200 acres

Closest Town: Ames

Iowa's forest floors begin blooming in March with spring beauty, bloodroot, trillium, and hepatica. By April, Dutchman's breeches, wild geranium, columbine, and sweet William begin to bloom. In May, the May apples unfold.

34. HENDRICKSON MARSH WILDLIFE AREA

Description: In a gently rolling landscape, this wetland is home to a large number of aquatic and grassland animals. More than 60 species of birds may nest here; grassland nesters include meadowlarks, dickcissels, grasshopper sparrows, bobolinks, and ring-necked pheasants. Willow flycatchers, common yellowthroats, northern orioles, yellow warblers, and warbling vireos can be found in the willow, silver maple, and cottonwood groves surrounding the marsh. Canada geese, mallards, and wood ducks all nest here, as do shorebirds such as killdeer and spotted sandpipers. Great blue herons and American white pelicans are common visitors, and great egrets and common loons occasionally are seen. During May and June, listen to the trill of the American toad and the varied night songs of chorus, leopard, and gray tree frogs.

Viewing Information: The best viewing of wildlife on the marsh is from the south-central parking lot. A good wildlife viewing trail begins on the west side of the area by the bridge; blue-winged teal and mallards summer at the pond at the trail's end. Bald eagles and ospreys often visit the marsh in March and April. Double-crested cormorants use transplanted poles as perches from late April to early June. During September and October large flocks of cliff, barn, tree, bank, and northern rough-winged swallows dive after insects close to the water's surface. Ring-billed gulls and black terns are also visible then. Thousands of snow geese use this area in March. Loggerhead shrikes not only nest here but can sometimes be found along hedgerows in the northwestern corner during winter. White-tailed deer and coyotes can be seen year-round. *USE CAUTION DURING FALL HUNTING SEASON.*

Directions: *At the intersection of U.S. Highways 30 and 65 at Colo, go south 7.2 miles on US 65; turn east at Collins on County Road E63 and follow it for 4.8 miles to the southwest corner of the marsh, or for 5.2 miles to the south-central parking lot, on the north side of CR E63.*

Ownership: IDNR (515) 752-5521

Size: 780 acres

Closest Town: Rhodes

During the 1890s, a button industry thrived along the Mississippi River. "Pearl buttons" were created from mussel shells. Unregulated harvesting and damming the river decreased many populations. Today some clams are still harvested—their shells are used to stimulate cultivated pearls.

35. HARDIN COUNTY GREENBELT

Description: This series of county-owned areas is located along the scenic Iowa River Valley. The valley is surrounded by oak- and hickory-covered bluffs with a few stands of native white pine and white birch. White-tailed deer, red foxes, woodchucks, beavers, and wild turkeys are residents. Nesting birds include barred owls, belted kingfishers, wood thrushes, cerulean warblers, American redstarts, and scarlet tanagers.

Viewing Information: The area can be viewed in several ways. The Iowa River Greenbelt Scenic Drive from Iowa Falls to Eldora is a great way to see the area by car. The river is also popular with canoeists. Write the Hardin CCB or the IDNR for a brochure on canoeing the Iowa River. Wild turkeys and white-tailed deer are commonly seen in fields along the river, especially in fall and winter. Bald eagles are also regularly seen along the river in fall and early winter. The area is known for spectacular fall colors, with the peak about October 10. Many woodland birds are found in the larger tracts of timber such as Pine Lake State Park, Mann Wilderness Area, and Leverton Timber. Migrant warblers, thrushes, and flycatchers are common at Pine Lake State Park in May. Check Upper Pine Lake in spring for migrant waterfowl. Deer abound in the park, and are seen at dusk in fields north of the park year-round. *USE CAUTION IN SOME AREAS DURING HUNTING SEASON.*

Directions: *Maps of the greenbelt may be obtained at the Hardin County Conservation Board Headquarters, located on the south side of the square in Eldora; Regular business hours are 9 a.m.-12 p.m. Monday-Friday.*

Ownership: Hardin County Conservation Board (515) 858-3461

Size: 1,500 acres

Closest Town: Eldora

Wooded greenbelts, such as Hardin County's, provide important homes and travelways for wildlife, plus control erosion and pesticide runoff. One-third of Iowa's 29,500 miles of perennial streams are protected for drinking water or recreation.

CARL KURTZ

PRAIRIE POTHOLE

REGION THREE: THE HEARTLAND

The Heartland includes the topographical areas of the Southern Iowa Drift Plain, Iowan Surface, and Mississippi Alluvial Plain. The area varies from steep, rolling hills in the southern plains to more gentle hills in the Iowan Surface.

Like much of the rest of the state, the area was once covered with rich glacial material and loess. These raw materials and the deep, interlaced prairie root system created some of the richest soil in the world.

In less than a century, most of Iowa's prairies were plowed under. By 1930, more than 95 percent of the state was in farmland. Iowa's soils continue to play an important role in the nation's food and energy production. Unfortunately, as much as half of the state's rich topsoil has already been washed away by erosion. Much of the erosion has occurred during the last 40 years with the advent of larger farms, monocrops of corn and soybeans, and elimination of grass rotations.

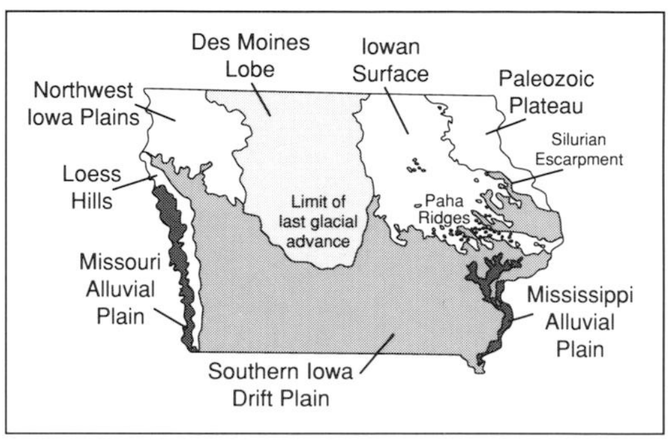

Viewing in this area ranges from human-engineered sites to quiet woodlands. Cedar Lake hosts a variety of wetland species; visitors may glimpse a peregrine falcon in downtown Cedar Rapids. During winter, bald eagles concentrate near the locks and dams of the Mississippi River, at reservoirs or along major, ice-free waterways. Bellevue State Park hosts one of the state's most famous butterfly gardens as well as woodlands overlooking the Mississippi River. Walnut Creek may some day be the world's largest reconstructed prairie, complete with bison. Bats hibernate in Maquoketa Caves and can be seen flying above the limestone cliffs at Palisades–Kepler State Park. Wild turkeys and deer can be seen at Stephen's State Forest, and waterfowl can be enjoyed at Riverton, Green Island, and Otter Creek. The Heartland is a diverse area, highly influenced by humans but still rich in wildlife viewing—and in promise.

Iowa farmland, spring.
KEVIN MAGEE

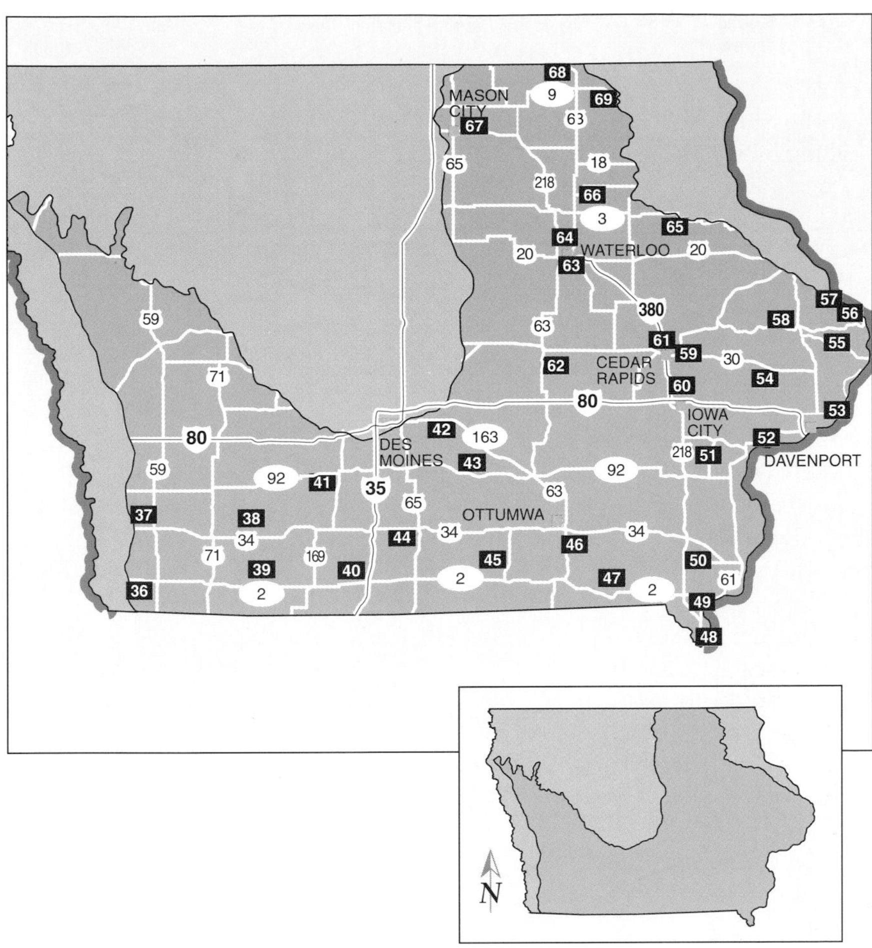

Wildlife Viewing Sites

36 Riverton Wildlife Area
37 Willow Slough Wildlife Area
38 Lake Icaria Recreation Area
39 Lake of Three Fires State Park
40 Sand Creek Wildlife Area
41 Pammel State Park
42 Walnut Creek NWR
43 Red Rock Lake and Wildlife Area
44 Stephen's State Forest
45 Rathbun Lake and Wildlife Area
46 Pioneer Ridge Nature Area
47 Lacey-Keosauqua State Park and Lake Sugema Wildlife Area
48 Lock and Dam 19
49 Heron Bend Conservation Area
50 Geode State Park
51 Cone Marsh Wildlife Area
52 Wildcat Den State Park
53 Lock and Dam 14
54 Wapsi River Environmental Education Center
55 Goose Lake Wildlife Area
56 Green Island Wildlife Area
57 Bellevue State Park
58 Maquoketa Caves State Park
59 Palisades-Kepler State Park
60 Coralville Lake and Wildlife Area
61 Cedar Lake
62 Otter Creek Marsh Wildlife Area
63 Hartman Reserve Nature Center
64 George Wyth Memorial State Park
65 Backbone State Park
66 Sweet Marsh Wildlife Area
67 Lime Creek Nature Center
68 Hayden Prairie State Preserve
69 Cardinal Marsh Wildlife Area

FARMLANDS AND WILDLIFE OF THE HEARTLAND

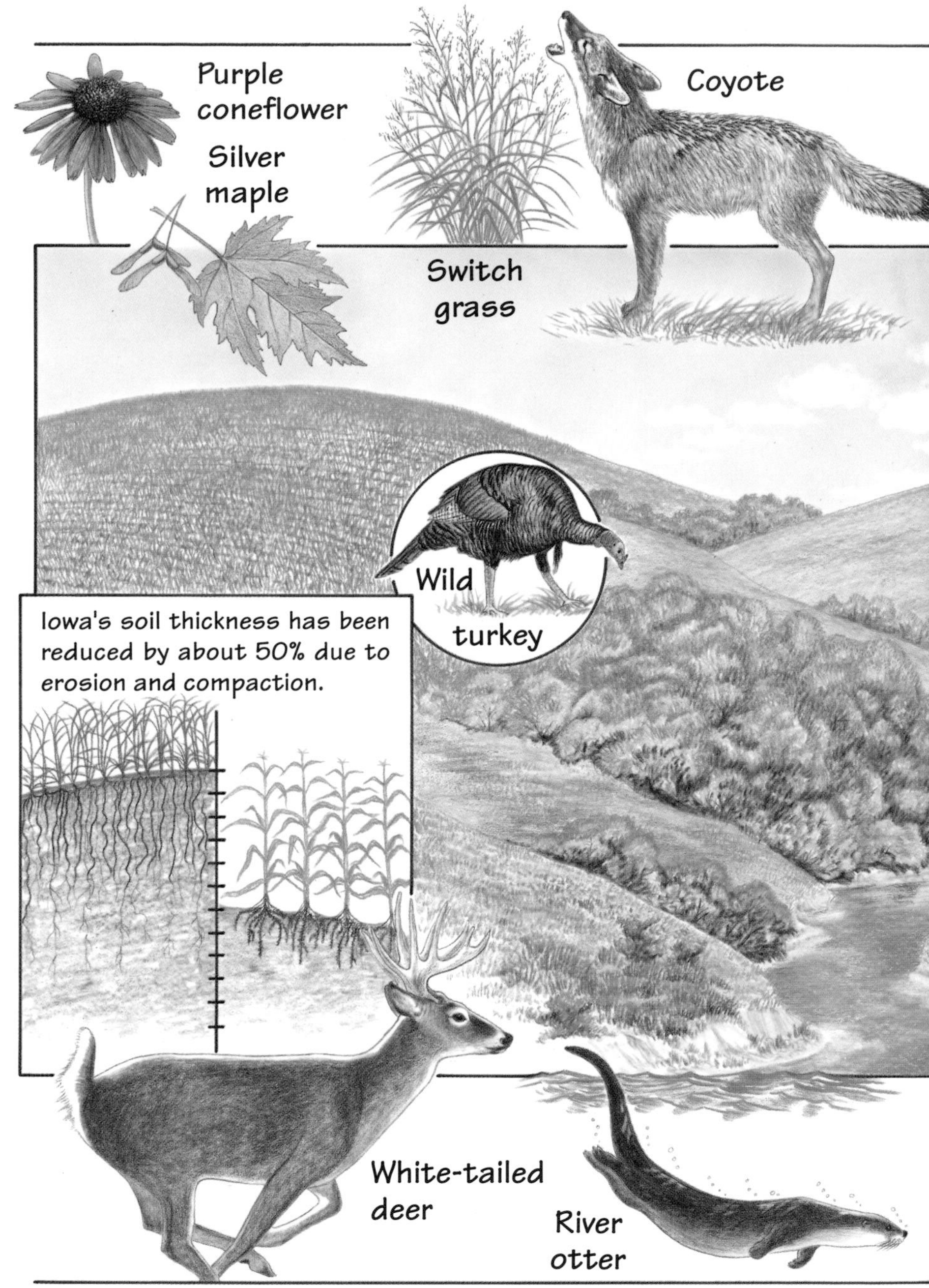

Wooded waterways provide important habitat and travel routes for wildlife. Throughout the Heartland, these riparian corridors provide viewing opportunities for colorful migrating warblers, herons, wild turkeys, and bald eagles. River otters were reintroduced in several of this region's rivers and reservoirs. Tree frogs sing throughout forest wetlands, and a smallmouth salamander may be found in the southern woodlands. All 9 species of Iowa's bats use woodlands and frequently hunt insects along river corridors.

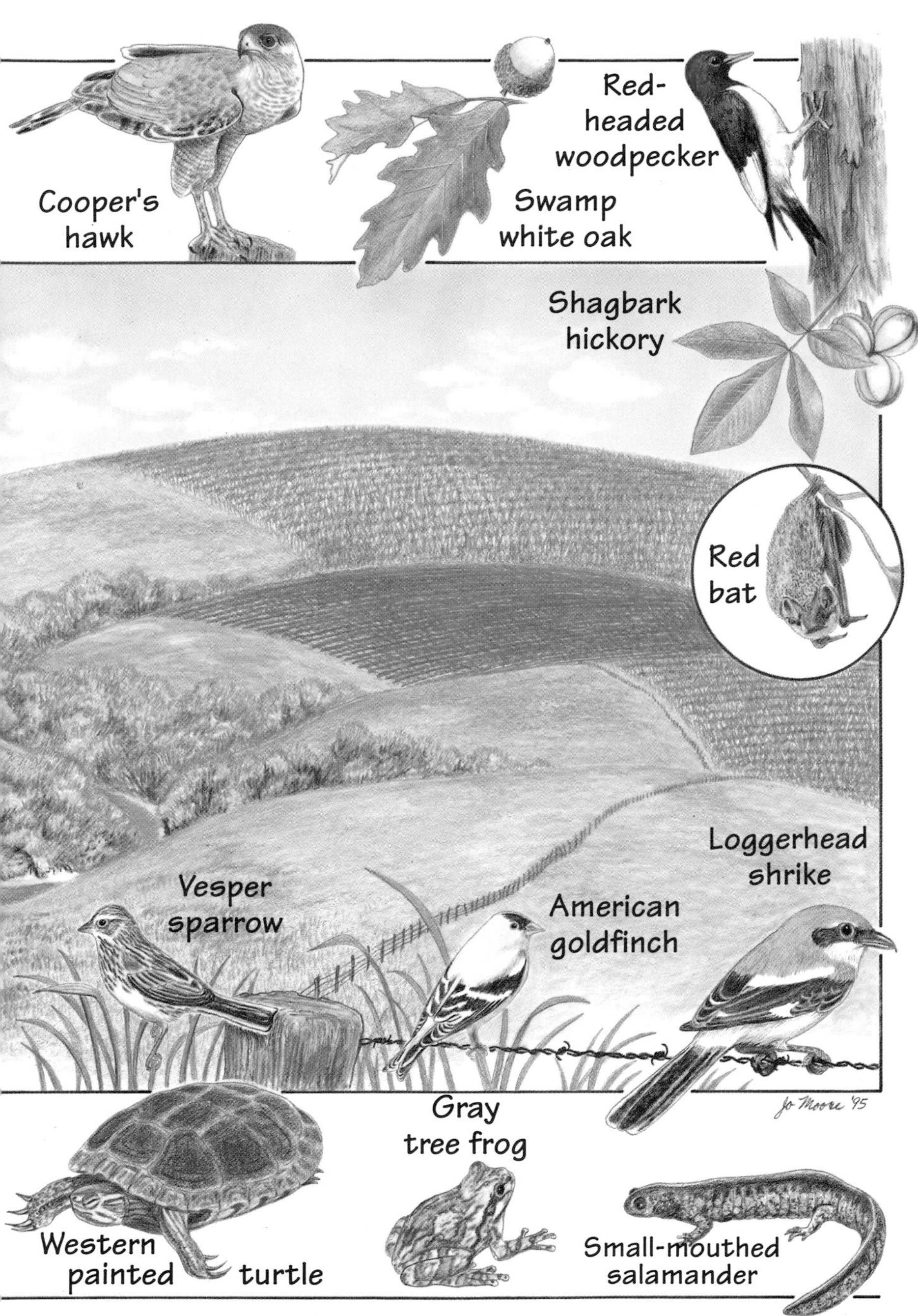

Loggerhead shrikes hunt from power lines and fences. Many steep hills in southern Iowa have been left as pasture, which provides habitat for upland sandpipers and hope for the reintroduction of greater prairie chickens. To control erosion, row crop areas need terraces, grassy drainages, adequate vegetative buffers along streams, and proper management. Sites 36, 43 and 48 offer excellent views of migrating waterfowl and bald eagles. A variety of woodland species can be enjoyed at Sites 44, 47, 52, and 65.

36. RIVERTON WILDLIFE AREA

Description: This large wetland is situated in the Nishnabotna River Valley. The habitats are varied, including marsh, upland and flooded timber, and open fields. The area is known for large concentrations of waterfowl, especially snow geese. Concentrations of bald eagles can be spectacular. From spring through late summer, large numbers of shorebirds may stop if water levels are suitable. Nesting birds include tree swallows, sedge wrens, prothonotary warblers, and eastern and western meadowlarks. White-tailed deer, wild turkeys, muskrats, beavers, red foxes, coyotes, and mink are residents.

Viewing Information: The observation deck is a great spot for viewing the upper reaches of the wetland. Except during the hunting season (September 15 through December 25), walk the numerous dikes for closer views. A gravel/paved lane winds along the north and west sides of the area, but may be impassable during wet weather and is closed during hunting season. Waterfowl peak in March and from October through November. Mallards, blue- and green-winged teal, and northern pintails are among the most common species. Thousands of snow geese are seen in March, though the peak is from late November to mid-December when concentrations may exceed 200,000 birds. Bald eagles peak from November through December with 50 or more present most years. Coyotes frequently are seen eating injured waterfowl in fall and winter. The spring migration of shorebirds can be excellent from April through May if water levels are low. Expect 20 or more species, including Hudsonian godwits, Baird's and stilt sandpipers, and Wilson's phalaropes. Snapping and painted turtles are common, and smallmouth salamanders are present but hard to observe. In late summer, look for shorebirds and several species of herons and egrets on mudflats. *USE CAUTION DURING HUNTING SEASON.*

Directions: *From the junction of Iowa Highway 2 and U.S. Highway 275 in Sidney, follow IA 2 east 4.2 miles and turn south on County Road L68. Proceed 2.6 miles and turn west at the headquarters for the Riverton Wildlife Unit. Immediately bear right and follow the paved road 0.4 mile to an observation deck.*

Ownership: IDNR (712) 374-3133

Size: 2,700 acres

Closest Town: Sidney

During fall, large groups of hawks, called kettles, can frequently be seen migrating along major river valleys. The river bluffs help produce wind currents that allow the hawks to soar extensively and save energy by not flapping their wings.

37. WILLOW SLOUGH WILDLIFE AREA

Description: This wetland, with adjacent bottomland forest and open fields, is known for large spring concentrations of waterfowl. Up to 50,000 snow geese, along with thousands of ducks, may be present. Nesting birds include pied-billed grebes, green herons, Canada geese, wood ducks, and Bell's vireos. During dry years, many shorebirds and herons may use the area from spring through late summer. This is one of the few spots in Iowa where massasauga rattlesnakes live. White-tailed deer, coyotes, red foxes, muskrats, beavers, and wild turkeys are residents.

Viewing Information: A dike circling much of the marsh offers excellent viewing . Waterfowl peak in March, and it is possible to see 20 species in a day, including greater white-fronted geese and northern pintail. Fewer waterfowl are present in fall because of hunting pressure. Wild turkeys and white-tailed deer are in the wooded area along the entrance road. Massasauga rattlesnakes are occasionally seen loafing on the dike in spring and summer. American white pelicans frequent the marsh in migration, especially during August and September. Watch for coyotes along the entrance road and dike, especially in winter. *USE CAUTION DURING HUNTING SEASON.*

Directions: *From the junction of U.S. Highway 34 and County Road M16 east of Hastings, follow CR M16 (370th Street) north 3.9 miles and turn east on Ellington Avenue. Drive 0.2 mile and turn north on Evarts Road. Follow Evarts Road north and east to the west end of the slough.*

Ownership: IDNR (712) 374-3133

Size: 599 acres **Closest Town:** Hastings

Observed statewide during migration, canvasback numbers peak at site 49 (Heron Bend Conservation Area) on the Mississippi River. Each spring and fall several thousand diving ducks may stop at Pool 19 to eat fingernail clams and wild celery. TY SMEDES

38. LAKE ICARIA RECREATION AREA

Description: This 700-acre lake surrounded by oak forest, grasslands, and brushy fields is known for large concentrations of Canada geese and other waterfowl during migration. White-tailed deer, red foxes, coyotes, and beavers are residents. Nesting birds include Canada geese, eastern kingbirds, eastern bluebirds, loggerhead shrikes, Bell's vireos, and field sparrows.

Viewing Information: A gravel road winds east along the north side of the lake with several places to view different sections of the lake. White-tailed deer are common along the wooded margins of the lake. The spring waterfowl migration is good from March through April with most of the common species plus snow geese using the lake. The fall waterfowl migration peaks in October and November when several thousand ducks and Canada geese may be present. In fall, waterfowl are concentrated in the refuge and goose pen just east of the park office. A few bald eagles also have been observed here at this time. *USE CAUTION DURING HUNTING SEASON.*

Directions: *From the junction of U.S. Highway 34 and Iowa Highway 148 in Corning, follow IA 148 north 5.9 miles and turn east at the entrance to the area. Proceed east 0.7 mile to a "T" intersection and turn north. Turn east immediately to the park office. A map of the area is available here.*

Ownership: IDNR (515) 464-2220

Size: 1,945 acres

Closest Town: Corning

One of Iowa's most familiar wildlife species, young raccoons are born in April or May and start following the female within 2 months. During the winter, they partially hibernate, but come out on warm days. DENVER BRYAN

39. LAKE OF THREE FIRES STATE PARK

Description: This park is known for the scenic oak-hickory bluffs surrounding 85-acre Lake of Three Fires. White-tailed deer, red foxes, coyotes, and fox squirrels are resident. Nesting birds include turkey vultures, wood ducks, barred owls, whip-poor-wills, wood thrushes, eastern bluebirds, and ovenbirds. The lake may have waterfowl and other aquatic birds during migration.

Viewing Information: Much of the park can be viewed from roads and more than 8 miles of trails. The trail along the west side of the lake passes through mature oak forest that is home to white-tailed deer, fox squirrels, and red-headed woodpeckers year-round. The marsh at the north end of the lake is best viewed from the campground. Expect nesting wood ducks and green herons, beavers, and some waterfowl during migration in March and October through November.

***Directions:** From the junction of Iowa Highways 2 and 148 South on the east edge of Bedford, follow IA 2 east 0.8 mile and turn north on Iowa Highway 49. Proceed 2.9 miles to the park entrance, on the left.*

Ownership: IDNR (712) 523-2700

Size: 694 acres

Closest Town: Bedford

40. SAND CREEK WILDLIFE AREA

Description: This undeveloped tract of oak forest offers visitors a true wilderness experience. Wild turkeys, white-tailed deer, red foxes, and mink are residents. Nesting birds include turkey vultures, northern bobwhites, eastern screech owls, red-headed woodpeckers, red-eyed vireos, and scarlet tanagers. The spring wildflower bloom is excellent.

Viewing Information: There are several mowed trails in the area, though much of the area is accessible only by hiking off the main trails. In April and May experience the wildflower bloom and warbler migration in the forest. White-tailed deer are abundant in spring and summer, but become more difficult to see during the fall hunting season. This area offers visitors the chance to easily view woodpeckers, tufted titmice, vireos, rose-breasted grosbeaks, and northern orioles. *USE CAUTION DURING HUNTING SEASON.*

***Directions:** From the junction of County Road J20 (East 1st Street) and County Road R15 (Riverside Street) in Grand River, follow CR J20 west 2.5 miles and turn north on a gravel road. Proceed 0.5 mile and turn west. Continue west 0.5 mile, then north another 0.5 mile to a parking area.*

Ownership: IDNR (515) 464-2220

Size: 2,600 acres

Closest Town: Grand River

41. PAMMEL STATE PARK

Description: Sacred, tranquil, picturesque—these words all describe this unique wooded area of limestone ridges overlooking the winding Middle River. During migration many species of warblers, vireos, and flycatchers can be seen flitting through the branches of old ridge-top white oak trees, which date back to the 1640s. The combination of upland and bottomland timber and oak savannah habitats contain a wide array of wildlife including about 70 different nesting birds. At dawn and dusk during April and May, witness the sky dance of the American woodcock, and in the evening listen to the night music of whip-poor-wills, barred owls, chorus frogs, and gray tree frogs. This is also the peak time for viewing woodland wildflowers.

Viewing information: Park maps showing hiking trails are available at the park office at the north entrance. During spring and summer, hike the backbone trail and watch the river below for great blue herons, green herons, wood duck families, beavers, and river otters. In the large wooded areas in the center of the park, listen and watch for scarlet tanagers, yellow-throated vireos, and ovenbirds. Small open areas throughout the park offer prime viewing of white-tailed deer, wild turkeys, fox squirrels, eastern chipmunks, red-headed woodpeckers, and occasionally a coyote or red or gray fox. Calls of the state-endangered bobcat have also been heard in the park. Watch for eastern bluebirds and black-capped chickadees using park nest boxes. A few timber rattlesnakes still survive amidst limestone outcroppings, so please give these rare Iowa reptiles a wide berth should you be fortunate enough to see them.

Directions: *From Winterset, drive west 1 mile on Iowa Highway 92 to where it intersects Iowa Highway 322. Turn south on IA 322 and drive 2.6 miles to the park entrance sign. The park office is on the left.*

Ownership: IDNR; managed by the Madison County Conservation Board (515) 462-3536

Size: 281 acres

Closest Town: Winterset

At twilight in Iowa, wild sounds can be heard: from great horned owls in January to screech owls in February, chorus frogs in March, turkeys in April, whip-poor-wills in May, and plains spadefoot toads in July.

42. WALNUT CREEK NATIONAL WILDLIFE REFUGE

Description: This refuge is currently in the development stage with a visitor center, trails, and other facilities scheduled to be completed in 1996. Today the refuge includes prairie and savannah remnants, planted prairie areas, and agricultural land. Restoration of nearly 5,000 acres of tallgrass prairie and oak savannah will be completed by the turn of the century. Resident species include white-tailed deer, red foxes, coyotes, and beavers. Bats are numerous in wooded ravines, including the endangered Indiana bat. Nesting birds include yellow-billed cuckoos, eastern kingbirds, sedge wrens, loggerhead shrikes, indigo buntings, dickcissels, and grasshopper sparrows.

Viewing Information: Check at the refuge headquarters for information on access. Most viewing is from a car, though visitors can hike to several areas. Savannah habitat in the southern half of the refuge is excellent for white-tailed deer. Bats are numerous in wooded ravines near creeks. Little brown myotis are common, and red and Indiana bats also are present.

Directions: *From Iowa Highway 163 in Prairie City, follow County Road S6G south 2 miles. Turn west on South 96th Avenue West and proceed 1 mile to West 109th Street South. Turn south and proceed 0.8 mile to the refuge headquarters, on the left. A visitor center will open in May 1996 and will be accessible from IA 163 via the Prairie City exit.*

Ownership: USFWS (515) 994-2415

Size: 5,000 acres

Closest Town: Prairie City

Since their reintroduction in the 1980s, river otters have now been observed in 51 counties throughout Iowa. Otters often use beaver lodges or logjams and may leave their tracks on sandbars or in the snow.

DENVER BRYAN

43. RED ROCK LAKE AND WILDLIFE AREA

Description: Located in the Des Moines River valley, this area contains a 19,000-acre reservoir surrounded by wooded bluffs and a variety of open habitats. The area is a haven for birds, with nearly 300 species recorded. Concentrations of 100,000 waterfowl occur in fall, along with large numbers of bald eagles. Migrant passerines are abundant. Nesting birds include wild turkeys, yellow-billed cuckoos, barred owls, eastern bluebirds, indigo buntings, and field sparrows. Resident mammals include white-tailed deer, red and gray foxes, coyotes, and river otters.

Viewing Information: The visitor center has an observation deck, wildlife displays and nature programs (call for dates). Memorial Day to Labor Day the center is open 9:30 a.m. to 6 p.m. Check the tailwater area and Howell Station Recreation Area from December through March for close views of wintering waterfowl and bald eagles. In November, thousands of gulls concentrate here, mostly ring-billed and herring gulls. The North and South Overlooks and White Breast Point offer good views of the reservoir. Expect waterfowl, loons, grebes, and cormorants during migration and coyotes on the ice in winter. The bay at Whitebreast may be low in late summer, providing habitat for great egret, several species of terns, and shorebirds. The wooded bluffs along the lake are excellent for migrant flycatchers, warblers, thrushes, and other passerines, and provide habitat for the abundant white-tailed deer. The west end of the reservoir is shallower, providing habitat for waterfowl, herons, American white pelicans, and shorebirds. View from the observation deck along Iowa Highway 316, 3.1 miles south of Runnells. During migration, expect large numbers of waterfowl. In March and from November through December, look for bald eagles perched in the trees along the river. American white pelicans occur in April and from August through September. Water levels often drop in late summer, creating habitat for shorebirds and herons. Watch for river otters here year-round. *USE CAUTION DURING HUNTING SEASON. SOME PORTIONS OF THE AREA ARE A REFUGE AND CLOSED FROM SEPTEMBER 15 THROUGH DECEMBER 25.*

Directions: *From Iowa Highway 163 west of Pella, take the Washington Street/Lake Red Rock exit (Exit 40). Follow the paved road west 0.7 mile and turn south on County Road T15. Proceed 3 miles to the Corps office and visitor center at the south end of the dam, where maps are available.*

Ownership: USACOE (515) 828-7522; IDNR (515) 961-0716

Size: 52,545 acres

Closest Town: Pella

44. STEPHEN'S STATE FOREST

Description: Much of this beautiful area is comprised of oak-hickory forest interspersed with old-growth fields and agricultural plantings. White-tailed deer, red foxes, coyotes, opossums, and wild turkeys are residents. Nesting birds include Cooper's hawks, ruffed grouse, barred owls, white-eyed vireos, blue-winged warblers, ovenbirds, and field sparrows.

Viewing Information: There is excellent viewing from roads and by hiking several miles of trails. Wild turkeys, white-tailed deer, and red foxes are common and are often seen along the road in early morning. In April, listen for drumming ruffed grouse, which were reintroduced to the area in 1972. Forest openings are home to nesting American woodcock. Along forest edge and in old-growth fields, look for nesting blue-winged warblers and field sparrows. On summer evenings, listen for whip-poor-wills and perhaps a chuck-will's-widow. It is worth a visit in October to see the fall colors. Raptors, including Cooper's, red-tailed, and rough-legged hawks, are present in winter. *USE CAUTION DURING HUNTING SEASON. ROADS MAY BE IMPASSABLE AFTER HEAVY RAINS.*

Directions: *From the junction of U.S. Highways 34 and 65 in Lucas, follow US 34 west 0.3 mile and turn south on a gravel road. Proceed 0.8 mile south and west to the Lucas Unit boundary. From here, the road winds south and west, passing several parking areas and a campground. Continue south through the Lucas Unit to a "T" intersection. Turn west and proceed 0.5 mile to the White Breast Unit.*

Ownership: IDNR (515) 774-5632

Size: 9,202 acres

Closest Town: Lucas

During migration, hundreds of American white pelicans may gather at large lakes and reservoirs such as Red Rock. With spectacular 9-foot wingspans, they fly in long, rolling, V-shaped lines. DeWAINE JACKSON

45. RATHBUN LAKE AND WILDLIFE AREA

Description: This area includes an 11,000-acre reservoir surrounded by oak-hickory forest and grassy fields. It is known for a diversity of birds with more than 275 species recorded. American white pelicans, waterfowl, bald eagles, shorebirds, gulls, and warblers and other passerines are seen in migration. Nesting birds include great blue herons, northern harriers, wild turkeys, willow flycatchers, tufted titmice, eastern bluebirds, and orchard orioles. Mammals that live here include white-tailed deer, coyotes, red foxes, beavers, mink, river otters, and muskrats.

Viewing Information: Be sure to get a wildlife auto tour guide pamphlet at the visitor center. This pamphlet highlights the best areas to view wildlife around the lake. Waterfowl are common March through April and October through December and may be seen anywhere around the lake, especially at the Colyn Wildlife Area near the Rathbun Unit headquarters. Thousands of scaup, ring-necked ducks, and mergansers often concentrate just above the dam. American white pelicans frequent the shallower western portion of the lake in April and September. Great blue herons are common during summer and nest near Woodpecker Marsh. Eastern bluebirds are summer residents around the lake. Wild turkeys are best seen at Honey Creek State Park in winter. Bald eagles may be seen from the dam to Honey Creek, especially in November and December, when as many as 30 may be present. Large numbers of raptors, including red-tailed and rough-legged hawks and northern harriers, are present in winter. *USE CAUTION IN SOME AREAS DURING HUNTING SEASONS.*

Directions: *From the junction of Iowa Highways 2 and 5 in Centerville, follow IA 5 north 3.7 miles and turn west on County Road J29. Proceed 3.8 miles to a "T" intersection. Turn north, then immediately left into the visitor center. Maps of the area are available here.*

Ownership: USACOE (515) 647-2464; IDNR (515) 774-4918

Size: 33,000 acres

Closest Town: Centerville

Six-foot-deep prairie plant roots helped to create Iowa's rich topsoil. Native prairies contained 60% grass, 35% forbs and 5% shrubs. Most prairie plants are perennials and can live 25 to 100 years. Prairies are resistant to droughts and flourish with occasional fires.

46. PIONEER RIDGE NATURE AREA

Description: This diverse area includes oak-hickory forest, old fields, native prairie, and several small ponds. The Nature Center has numerous wildlife exhibits and a bird-feeding operation. White-tailed deer and wild turkeys are resident. Red foxes are occasionally seen. Nesting birds include northern bobwhites, whip-poor-wills, white-eyed vireos, blue-winged and Kentucky warblers, rufous-sided towhees, and field sparrows.

Viewing Information: The area contains more than 15 miles of trails that provide an excellent way to view the area's wildlife. In summer, look for ruby-throated hummingbirds at the hummingbird feeders at the Nature Center. White-tailed deer are numerous and are easily seen in fields around the Nature Center at dusk. Wild turkeys are also common and are often seen along park trails. Wood ducks frequent the small ponds in spring and summer. The area has a variety of songbirds and is good for migrant flycatchers, thrushes, and warblers in May and September.

Directions: *From the junction of U.S. Highways 34 and 63 in Ottumwa, follow US 63 south for 6.9 miles to the entrance on the left. A map of the area is available at the Nature Center.*

Ownership: Wapello County Conservation Board (515) 682-3091

Size: 737 acres

Closest Town: Ottumwa

Famous for large winter concentrations at dams along the Mississippi River, bald eagles also concentrate at reservoirs and other ice-free rivers. More than 30 pairs of eagles nest in Iowa each summer. RICHARD DAY

47. LACEY–KEOSAUQUA STATE PARK AND LAKE SUGEMA WILDLIFE AREA

Description: This large complex includes a state park and wildlife area as well as the adjacent Keosauqua Unit of Shimek State Forest. This scenic area contains oak-hickory covered bluffs bordering the Des Moines River, as well as grasslands and some restored prairie. White-tailed deer, red and gray foxes, beavers, and wild turkeys are resident. Nesting birds include turkey vultures, Acadian flycatchers, Carolina wrens, eastern bluebirds, northern mockingbirds, northern parulas, yellow-throated and Kentucky warblers, Louisiana waterthrushes, and summer and scarlet tanagers. The area is also known for a diversity of migrant thrushes and warblers. Several species of bats, including the Indiana bat, have been observed in the area.

Viewing Information: Ely Ford is a good place to see nesting Acadian flycatchers, blue-gray gnatcatchers, northern parulas, and yellow-throated warblers from April to July. The trail from Ely Ford east to the park entrance offers views of the river valley. In fall and winter look for bald eagles, and scan the river for swallows in summer. During summer at the campground, listen for ovenbirds and summer and scarlet tanagers. Wild turkeys are seen year-round along park roads. Lake Sugema Wildlife Area contains a 575-acre lake surrounded by a variety of open habitats. Expect to see a variety of water birds including cormorants, herons, and waterfowl in migration. Canada geese, mallards, and wood ducks nest here. Great blue and green herons perch in flooded trees in spring and summer. In summer, the weedy fields around the lake are home to northern bobwhites, Bell's vireos, grasshopper and Henslow's sparrows, and bobolinks. *USE CAUTION DURING HUNTING SEASONS.*

Directions: *From the town of Keosauqua, follow Iowa Highway 1 south across the Des Moines River and turn west at the park entrance. Proceed west for 1.5 miles to the campground. Maps of the park and nearby Lake Sugema are available here.*

Ownership: IDNR (319) 293-3502

Size: 6,169 acres

Closest Town: Keosauqua

The Breeding Bird Atlas was Iowa's first statewide bird survey. The 10 most widely distributed birds documented were: house sparrow, red-winged blackbird, American robin, mourning dove, brown-headed cowbird, barn swallow, common grackle, house wren, dickcissel, and eastern kingbird.

48. LOCK AND DAM 19

Description: This dam on the Mississippi River is probably one of the best sites in the interior United States to view wintering bald eagles, with as many as 300 present.

Viewing Information: The best eagle viewing is from the lock and dam site December through March. Walk across the lock toward the power plant, pass through a gate, and view from the sidewalk that overlooks the tailwaters (the gate is open Monday through Friday, 8 a.m. - 5 p.m.). Eagles may also be seen along the riverfront, south to Hubinger Landing. In winter, up to 35,000 American crows gather in trees along the riverfront before roosting in town.

Directions: *From the junction of 7th Street (U.S. Highway 136) and Main Street (U.S. Highway 218) in Keokuk, follow Main St. south for 5 blocks to 2nd Street, which is just before the bridge across the river to Illinois. Turn right on 2nd St. and go 3 blocks to Bank Street. Turn left and follow this road to a "T" intersection at the river. Turn north and proceed 0.3 mile to the Lock and Dam site. Or, turn south and drive a short distance to Hubinger Landing and a public boat ramp for good views of the river.*

Ownership: USACOE (309) 794-5338; call for dates of eagle watching events

Size: 7 acres

Closest Town: Keokuk

49. HERON BEND CONSERVATION AREA

Description: Scenic Pool 19 on the Mississippi River is an important resting spot for migrant waterfowl, with as many as 400,000 birds of various species recorded at the fall peak. Canvasbacks and lesser scaup are the most common, though nearly 20 other species of waterfowl may be seen here. This is also a good spot to view migrant and wintering bald eagles.

Viewing Information: In spring and fall from the boat ramp, spectacular numbers of waterfowl concentrate on the pool. Most of the common waterfowl species can be seen, as can American white pelicans, great egrets, bald eagles, and Bonaparte's gulls. In winter, bald eagles are numerous, and some waterfowl may linger during mild winters. In summer, look for American white pelicans, great blue herons, and great egrets in the marshy area northeast of the boat ramp. *USE CAUTION DURING HUNTING SEASON.*

Directions: *From the junction of U.S. Highway 61 and Iowa Highway 404 at the east edge of Montrose, follow US 61 north for 3.6 miles to the entrance on the right. Linger Longer Rest Area is located at the junction of US 61 and Iowa Highway 998, 2.1 miles south of Heron Bend.*

Ownership: Lee County Conservation Board (319) 463-7673

Size: 302 acres

Closest Town: Montrose

50. GEODE STATE PARK

Description: Nesting birds at this scenic park include wild turkeys, barred owls, whip-poor-wills, wood thrushes, northern parulas, ovenbirds, and scarlet tanagers. White-tailed deer, gray foxes, and raccoons are residents. The park is also home to timber rattlesnakes and bullfrogs.

Viewing Information: More than 4 miles of trails encircle the lake. In April, listen for wild turkeys gobbling in the bluffs. May is the peak time to see migrant flycatchers, thrushes, vireos, and warblers. The trail along the north and west sides of the lake passes through mature oak forest with breeding Acadian flycatchers, wood thrushes, ovenbirds, and scarlet tanagers. From the small parking lot at the northeast end of the lake, listen for whip-poor-wills, American toads, and bullfrogs on summer evenings.

Directions: *From the junction of U.S. Highway 34 and Iowa Highway 79 in Middletown, follow IA 79 west for 5.8 miles to the park entrance. Continue another 0.4 mile to the campground, where a park map is available.*

Ownership: IDNR (319) 392-4601

Size: 1,641 acres

Closest Town: New London

51. CONE MARSH WILDLIFE AREA

Description: This large wetland complex is situated between the Iowa and Cedar rivers and is known for its diversity of birds. More than 250 species have been observed here, including such nesting species as American woodcock, barred owl, willow flycatcher, prothonotary warbler, and yellow-headed blackbird. White-tailed deer, red and gray foxes, beavers, and mink are residents.

Viewing Information: The majority of Cone Marsh is private property, so be careful not to trespass. Much of the private property can be viewed from the road. For good views, hike the main dike east from the parking lot. View waterfowl in March and April, including greater white-fronted and snow geese. Spring is also good for migrant rails and shorebirds, the latter when water levels are low. American woodcock display in fields north of the parking lot in March and April. *USE CAUTION DURING HUNTING SEASON.*

Directions: *From the junction of Iowa Highway 70 and 1st Street in Conesville, follow 1st Street (which becomes 220th Street) west for 2.4 miles to the marsh, on both sides of the road (AT THIS POINT, THE MARSH IS PRIVATE PROPERTY, SO VIEW FROM THE ROAD). Continue west 1 mile and turn north on V Avenue. Proceed 0.6 mile to a parking lot on the right. From here, walk east on the main dike for views of the area.*

Ownership: IDNR (319) 523-8319

Size: 701 acres

Closest Town: Conesville

52. WILDCAT DEN STATE PARK

Description: This park consists of oak-hickory bluffs broken by steep ravines. Several trails provide scenic views of spectacular ravines within the park. The park is known for its diversity of warblers and other songbirds. White-tailed deer, red foxes, and opossums are residents.

Viewing Information: Viewing is from park roads and more than 2 miles of trails, including the scenic 1.5-mile Wildcat Den Interpretive Trail. Numerous ferns and wildflowers can be seen along this trail, especially in May. In May, as many as 20 species of warblers can be seen on a good day. In summer, nesting birds along the trail include eastern phoebes, wood thrushes, ovenbirds, and scarlet tanagers. White-tailed deer are commonly seen from park roads. Raccoons are almost certain to be seen at night during summer.

Directions: *From the junction of Iowa Highway 22/Iowa Highway 38/U.S. Highway 61 Business in Muscatine, follow IA 22 (also Washington Street and Great River Road) east for 9.5 miles and turn north at the sign for the park. Proceed north 0.8 mile to the park entrance. Obtain a park map at the park office.*

Ownership: IDNR (319) 263-4337

Size: 417 acres

Closest Town: Muscatine

53. LOCK AND DAM 14

Description: This large dam on the Mississippi River is noted for concentrations of wintering bald eagles and migrant waterfowl. As many as 100 eagles are present each winter. Wintering waterfowl include common goldeneyes and common mergansers. Large numbers of gulls, mostly herring and ring-billed gulls, feed below the dam during migration.

Viewing Information: View the area from the boat launch. Eagles are present from November to March and are seen feeding below the dam and roosting in trees along the river's edge. Peak numbers of bald eagles are present from December through February. Migrant waterfowl occur in March and from October through November, with a few wintering here. Gulls peak in November when thousands may be present. Summer viewing is less productive, but expect to see great blue herons and several swallow species, including purple martin.

Directions: *From Interstate 80, take the LeClaire/Iowa Highway 67 exit (Exit 306). Follow IA 67 south 2.7 miles and turn east on 181st Street. Proceed across the railroad tracks and immediately north on 182nd Street. Proceed 0.3 mile to the Lock and Dam Recreation Area, on the right.*

Ownership: USACOE (309) 794-5338; call for dates of eagle watching events.

Size: 100 acres

Closest Town: LeClaire

Eastern bluebirds return to Iowa in March and April. In 7 years, volunteers from across the state have helped to fledge more than 50,000 young bluebirds from nest boxes. RICHARD DAY

54. WAPSI RIVER ENVIRONMENTAL EDUCATION CENTER

Description: Situated along the Wapsipinicon River, this area is mostly covered by oak-hickory forest. The Education Center, is a joint project of Scott and Clinton counties and is open weekends from 1 p.m. to 5 p.m. Nearly 140 species of birds have been seen here. Mammals include white-tailed deer, red foxes, and several species of bats. At least 11 species of rare plants and animals have been recorded in the area.

Viewing Information: Bald eagles occur during winter. The woods are good for migrant warblers, sparrows, and other passerines. On summer evenings, listen for whip-poor-wills and watch for little brown myotis bats around the center.

Directions: *From the junction of U.S. Highway 30 and County Road Y4E (130th Avenue) in Wheatland, follow CR Y4E south 6 miles and turn north on 52nd Avenue. Follow signs to area. Sherman Park lies east of the Education Center on the east side of the Wapsipinicon River. From 52nd Avenue south of the Center, follow 310th Street east 0.5 mile and turn north on 57th Avenue. Proceed 1.5 miles to the park entrance on the left.*

Ownership: Clinton County Conservation Board (319) 847-7202; Scott County Conservation Board (319) 381-1114

Size: 407 acres

Closest town: Wheatland

THE HEARTLAND

55. GOOSE LAKE WILDLIFE AREA

Description: This is one of the largest natural marshes in eastern Iowa. The area is good for migrant waterfowl and nesting marsh birds such as Canada geese, wood ducks, common moorhens, marsh wrens, and yellow-headed blackbirds. Green frogs, mink, and muskrats are residents.

Viewing Information: Best viewing is from the dike that bisects the marsh. Look for migrant waterfowl in March and April, with the majority being puddle ducks. In summer, look for nesting yellow-headed blackbirds north of the dike. Nesting marsh birds are most numerous in the larger marsh south of the dike. Muskrats are abundant, and an occasional mink is seen along the marsh edge. In recent years, a pair of sandhill cranes has summered here and may nest in the area. In late summer, watch for least bittern and duck broods at dusk and shorebirds on mudflats north of the dike. *USE CAUTION DURING HUNTING SEASON.*

Directions: *From the junction of Iowa Highway 136 and County Road Z34 in the town of Goose Lake, follow IA 136 west for 1.7 miles and turn north on 350th Avenue. Proceed 0.5 mile and turn east on a gravel lane that leads to a parking area.*

Ownership: IDNR (319) 354-8343

Size: 893 acres **Closest town:** Goose Lake

56. GREEN ISLAND WILDLIFE AREA

Description: This area lies at the confluence of the Mississippi and Maquoketa rivers and features a 2,500-acre wetland surrounded by oak-covered bluffs. The area is known for large numbers of waterfowl and for migrant and wintering bald eagles. Nesting birds include wood ducks, hooded mergansers, turkey vultures, bald eagles, common moorhens, sandhill cranes, marsh wrens, and prothonotary warblers. Mammals include white-tailed deer, red and gray foxes, coyotes, muskrats, river otters, and raccoons. Black rat snakes, tiger salamanders, and gray tree frogs also have been seen here.

Viewing Information: Viewing is from the gravel road west of the headquarters and from the roads north to Blakes Lake and Fish Lake. Look for waterfowl in March and April, including large numbers of puddle ducks and Canada geese. Great blue herons, great egrets, and numerous shorebirds stop here during migration and summer, especially if one of the impoundments is low. In June and July, look for broods of wood ducks, hooded mergansers, and common moorhens. The bluff overlook provides spectacular views of the Mississippi River valley and is a good spot to view migrant raptors from September through October and bald eagles from November to March. *USE CAUTION DURING HUNTING SEASON.*

Directions: *From the junction of U.S. Highway 52/Iowa Highway 64/U.S. Highway 67 on the west edge of Sabula, follow US 52 north for 6.2 miles and turn north on Green Island Road (540th Avenue). Proceed 1.2 miles to the Maquoketa Unit headquarters, on the left. To reach the Green Island Bluff overlook, park in the lot across from the Maquoketa Unit headquarters. Follow the Nature Trail 0.4 mile to the top of the bluff and turn right to the bluff overlook.*

Ownership: IDNR (319) 652-3132

Size: 3,722 acres

Closest Town: Sabula

P

Partnerships with hunting and non-hunting conservation groups have been invaluable. In Iowa, these partnerships have helped acquire land, reintroduce native wildlife, and purchase equipment for wildlife research, management, and educational activities.

57. BELLEVUE STATE PARK

Description: This park is situated on high bluffs overlooking the Mississippi River. Much of the park is mixed hardwood forest, though there are numerous woodland openings and prairies. The highlight of the park is the butterfly garden, just southwest of the Nature Center. The birdlife of the park is varied with nesting birds like wild turkeys, pileated woodpeckers, Acadian flycatchers, red-eyed vireos, ovenbirds, and scarlet tanagers. Migrant thrushes, vireos, and warblers are common. White-tailed deer and red foxes are residents.

Viewing Information: The butterfly garden attracts numerous species of butterflies from May to September, including monarch, painted lady, red admiral, and swallowtail. Bats are frequently seen around the garden at dusk in summer. The park contains more than 10 miles of trails that traverse the area's habitats. There are spectacular views of the Mississippi River valley from the shelter at the head of Bluff Trail in the Dyas Unit. View migrant raptors here in September and October. Pileated woodpeckers and other species live here throughout the park; Deer and Duck Creek trails are especially worth hiking. Bald eagles winter at nearby Lock and Dam 12 on the Mississippi River and may be viewed from the park.

Directions: *From the junction of U.S. Highway 52 and Iowa Highway 62 (State Street) in Bellevue, follow US 52 south for 0.7 mile to the entrance of the Nelson Unit of Bellevue State Park, on the right. Follow the signs to the Nature Center to obtain a park map.*

Ownership: IDNR (319) 872-4019

Size: 547 acres **Closest Town:** Bellevue

Bellevue State Park hosts one of the state's largest butterfly gardens. Although spicebush swallowtails like this one are rare, numerous other butterfly species may be seen at Bellevue from spring through early fall. CARL KURTZ

58. MAQUOKETA CAVES STATE PARK

Description: The park contains 13 caves, more than any other park in Iowa. Many caves are lighted for easier viewing. The caves are important for bats, including eastern pipistrelles, little brown myotis, and big browns. White-tailed deer, red and gray foxes, raccoons, and wild turkeys are residents. Nesting birds include barred owls, blue-gray gnatcatchers, wood thrushes, yellow-throated vireos, and scarlet tanagers.

Viewing Information: While some of the park can be seen from a car, the best viewing is from more than 6 miles of trails. View spring wildflowers in April and May. From June through September, view bats as they exit the caves at dusk. Nesting birds are found along the nature trail south of the concession area in June.

Directions: *From the junction of U.S. Highway 61 and Iowa Highway 428 on the northwest side of Maquoketa, follow IA 428 west for 4.7 miles and turn west on 98th Street (still IA 428). Proceed a short distance to the park entrance. A park map is available at the restroom area just past the entrance.*

Ownership: IDNR (319) 652-5833

Size: 272 acres

Closest Town: Maquoketa

59. PALISADES–KEPLER STATE PARK

Description: This park lies along the beautiful Cedar River, flanked by limestone bluffs. White-tailed deer, opossums, raccoons, and wild turkeys are resident. Bats are common during summer. Nesting birds include wood ducks, Acadian flycatchers, blue-gray gnatcatchers, yellow-throated and red-eyed vireos, American redstarts, and scarlet tanagers.

Viewing Information: The trail along the Cedar River is worth walking for the scenery. The rocky bluffs and steep ravines are breathtaking, and are home to a variety of wildlife, including nesting Acadian flycatchers. Bald eagles frequent the river during migration and in winter. The park is an excellent place to view bats, including big browns and little brown myotis, especially around the campground and along the Cedar River. Large numbers of softshell turtles may be seen sunning on sandbars below the lowhead dam in summer.

Directions: *From the junction of Iowa Highway 1 and U.S. Highway 30 in Mount Vernon, follow US 30 west for 3.7 miles and turn south at the park entrance. Obtain a map of the area at the park office.*

Ownership: IDNR (319) 895-6039

Size: 840 acres

Closest Town: Mount Vernon

60. CORALVILLE LAKE AND WILDLIFE AREA

Description: This 5,430-acre reservoir is located in the Iowa River Valley and is home to more than 275 species of birds. The lake attracts migrant loons, grebes, American white pelicans, herons, waterfowl, shorebirds, and gulls. Nesting birds include double-crested cormorants, great blue herons, cliff swallows, eastern bluebirds, yellow-throated vireos, blue-winged warblers, American redstarts, lark sparrows, and northern orioles. White-tailed deer, red foxes, coyotes, mink, and wild turkeys are residents.

Viewing Information: The visitor center offers interpretive displays (call for hours). Migrant loons, grebes, waterfowl, gulls, and terns may be seen anywhere on the lake, though Jolly Roger, Swan Lake, and the Hawkeye Wildlife Area are probably the best sites. The Hawkeye Wildlife Area has large numbers of waterfowl in March and October through November. Viewing is from the shoulder of Iowa Highway 965 on the northeast side. Nesting double-crested cormorants can be seen here in summer, and American white pelicans are often here in April and August through September. In late summer, Swan Lake and parts of the Hawkeye Wildlife Area may have exposed mudflats that attract hundreds of shorebirds including semipalmated plovers, lesser yellowlegs, pectoral sandpipers, and both dowitchers, as well as great blue herons and great egrets. Bald eagles are seen around the lake in migration and a few winter on the Iowa River below the dam. Lake Macbride State Park is good for migrant warblers and other passerines, as well as breeding yellow-throated warblers and scarlet tanagers. Ask for directions to the Macbride Raptor Center exhibits for a close-up view of various hawks and owls. *USE CAUTION IN SOME AREAS DURING HUNTING SEASON.*

Directions: *From Interstate 80 in Iowa City, take the Dubuque Street exit (Exit 244). Follow Dubuque St. north for 2.6 miles and turn east on NE West Overlook Road. Proceed across the dam and follow signs to the visitor center. Obtain a map of the area here.*

Ownership: USACOE (319) 338-3543; IDNR (319) 354-8343

Size: 34,000 acres

Closest Town: Iowa City

Money raised from license fees and an excise tax on hunting equipment has helped purchase 324 wildlife areas totalling more than 255,000 acres. These wildlife areas represent nearly half of Iowa's public lands. Wildlife viewing is excellent on most of these sites.

THE HEARTLAND

61. CEDAR LAKE

Description: This urban lake attracts a diversity of waterfowl and other aquatic birds during migration and in winter. The warm water outflow from a generating station keeps part of the lake open all winter, attracting hundreds of ducks and Canada geese. A few loons, grebes, gulls, and terns use the lake during migration.

Viewing Information: The lake is owned by IES Utilities, Inc., but is leased to the City of Cedar Rapids for use as a park. Large numbers of swallows, mostly barn and cliff swallows, may gather here in August. Ospreys are occasionally seen fishing over the lake in fall. Peregrine falcons may nest in downtown Cedar Rapids and often use one nest site that allows close-up viewing via a television monitor. Call the IDNR, (515) 432-2823, for peregrine information.

Directions: *From Interstate 380 in downtown Cedar Rapids, drive north and take the exit for H and J Avenues (Exit 21). Turn south on H Ave., cross the railroad tracks, and turn east on Shaver Road NE, then immediately turn south into Cedar Lake Park.*

Ownership: City of Cedar Rapids (319) 398-5080

Size: 120 acres

Closest Town: Cedar Rapids

62. OTTER CREEK MARSH WILDLIFE AREA

Description: This large wetland is situated along the Iowa River. More than 240 species of birds have been seen here. Nesting birds include great blue herons, sandhill cranes, willow flycatchers, tree swallows, sedge wrens, American redstarts, and yellow-headed blackbirds. Mammals include white-tailed deer, river otters, red foxes, coyotes, and muskrats. Bullfrogs and American toads are summer residents.

Viewing Information: The extensive system of dikes provides good access to the area. Muskrat and mink are regularly seen. Waterfowl peak in March and April and are dominated by puddle ducks such as mallard and blue-winged teal. Look for river otters on the larger pools at the east end of the marsh. Great blue herons nest along the Iowa River. Sandhill cranes have nested here recently and are often seen feeding in fields along the north side of the area from April to November. *USE CAUTION DURING HUNTING SEASON.*

Directions: *From the junction of U.S. Highways 30 and 63 in Toledo, follow US 30 east for 7.4 miles and turn south on County Road E66. Proceed southeast for 2.9 miles and turn south on S Avenue. Proceed 0.4 mile to a parking area on right.*

Ownership: IDNR (515) 489-2574 or (515) 752-5521

Size: 3,400 acres

Closest Town: Toledo/Tama

63. HARTMAN RESERVE NATURE CENTER

Description: The Hartman Reserve Nature Center is open Monday through Friday, 8 a.m. - 4:30 p.m., and 1 p.m. - 5 p.m. on Sundays and has displays of local fauna. White-tailed deer, red foxes, red and fox squirrels, and raccoons are residents. Nesting birds include wood ducks, Swainson's hawks, yellow-billed cuckoos, rose-breasted grosbeaks, and indigo buntings.

Viewing Information: Hike more than 5 miles of trails through extensive hardwood forest, open meadows, prairie, and sloughs. The spring wildflower bloom is good from April through May. The forest is home to migrant warblers, thrushes, and other passerines in May and September. A pair of Swainson's hawks has nested here for 18 years, east of its normal range.

Directions: *From U.S. Highway 218 in Cedar Falls, take the Greenhill Road exit. Proceed west 0.2 mile and turn west on Rainbow Drive. Proceed west 0.9 mile and turn north on Laurie Avenue. Proceed 1 block to Grand Boulevard and turn west. Proceed another block and turn north on Timber Drive. Proceed 0.2 mile and turn north on Reserve Drive to Nature Center.*

Ownership: Black Hawk County Conservation Board (319) 277-2187

Size: 287 acres

Closest Town: Cedar Falls/Waterloo

64. GEORGE WYTH MEMORIAL STATE PARK

Description: This urban park lies along the Cedar River and is known for its large population of white-tailed deer. It's also a birder's favorite with more than 250 species recorded. The main attraction is the spring migration of warblers and other passerines. Spring peeper frogs and the endangered blue-spotted salamander are also present.

Viewing Information: Much of the park is accessible by car, with a 5-mile multipurpose trail providing access to areas along the Cedar River. Spring migration of warblers and other passerines peaks in May. The resident herd of 60 to 70 white-tailed deer is easily seen in fall and winter in open areas along the road at the east end of the park.

Directions: *From U.S. Highway 218 in Waterloo, take the George Wyth Memorial State Park exit. Turn south at the exit, then immediately west into the park. Park maps are available at the park office.*

Ownership: IDNR (319) 232-5505

Size: 494 acres

Closest Town: Waterloo

65. BACKBONE STATE PARK

Description: Backbone was Iowa's first state park, named for its 400-million-year-old ridge of dolomite limestone rising 100 feet above the Maquoketa River. The rocky, rugged, wooded terrain comprises spring-fed streams, caves, stately old native white pines, massive oak trees, and a great variety of plant and wildlife species. The Iowa-endangered red-shouldered hawk nests here; bald eagles can be seen fishing on the lake in spring and fall. Field studies indicate at least 87 types of birds reside in the park during summer. In the heart of the park where the forest is older, watch and listen for pileated woodpeckers, scarlet tanagers, whip-poor-wills, and wild turkeys. On sun-drenched rocky outcrops watch for a basking five-lined skink or a black rat snake. Woodland wildflowers are a special treat from April through June.

Viewing Information: This site has 28 miles of marked trails, boating on the lake, and many miles of roads, allowing access to all areas. Maps and general information are available at park headquarters. White-tailed deer, fox squirrels, raccoons, and eastern chipmunks are common throughout the park. Daytime insect feeders such as cliff and northern rough-winged swallows and purple martins can be seen over the lake behind the concession stand. In evening hours they are replaced by flying bats such as the little brown myotis and eastern pipistrelle. During spring evenings, visitors are serenaded by spring peepers, chorus, and green frogs; at dawn listen for drumming ruffed grouse and watch for sky-dancing American woodcock. Canoeing at dawn or dusk is an excellent way to encounter swimming beavers, muskrats, and wood ducks. *PUBLIC HUNTING IS ALLOWED IN THE BACKBONE FOREST AREA AT NORTH END OF PARK. USE CAUTION DURING HUNTING SEASONS.*

Directions: *From the junction of Iowa Highway 3 and County Road W69 south of Strawberry Point, proceed 3.1 miles south on CR W69; then turn west on blacktop and travel 1.2 miles to park headquarters, on the south side of the road.*

Ownership: IDNR (319) 924-2527

Size: 1,780 acres (includes 100-acre artificial lake)

Closest Towns: Dundee, Strawberry Point

Roads in most of Iowa's state parks are suitable for bicycling. Iowa has also converted many miles of abandoned railroad lines to trails. These trails offer excellent wildlife viewing in addition to bicycling.

66. SWEET MARSH WILDLIFE AREA

Description: This large area includes open marsh, flooded bottomland forest, ponds, wet prairie, and oak savannah. These varied habitats make this an excellent birding site with more than 260 species recorded. The wetlands attract waterfowl and other aquatic birds, while wooded areas harbor migrant warblers and other passerines. Nesting birds include great blue and green herons, wood ducks, red-shouldered hawks, wild turkeys, tree swallows, American redstarts, and yellow-headed blackbirds. Mammals include white-tailed deer, river otters, mink, beavers, and red and gray foxes. Painted and softshell turtles, green and bullfrogs, and state-endangered massasauga rattlesnakes are also present.

Viewing Information: The area is accessible by car from all sides. Best viewing is by hiking the numerous dikes. Expect up to 20 species of waterfowl in March and April. Grebes, herons, bald eagles, rails, and shorebirds also pass through during migration. In May, wooded areas are excellent for migrant flycatchers, warblers, thrushes, vireos, and other passerines. River otters are present in the marsh, but difficult to see. Mink, muskrats, and beavers may be seen along dikes, especially in spring. A pair of red-shouldered hawks nests along the Wapsi River Greenbelt. Watch for migrant raptors in September and October. *USE CAUTION DURING HUNTING SEASON.*

Directions: *From the junction of Iowa Highway 93 and County Road C28 (7th Avenue SE) in Tripoli, follow CR C28 (which becomes 165th Street) east 1.8 miles. Cross the Wapsipinicon River, and turn north into the south end of the area. The Wapsi River Greenbelt, run by the Bremer County Conservation Board (319) 882-4742, is south of the marsh off 165th St.*

Ownership: IDNR (319) 422-5832

Size: 2,242 acres

Closest Town: Tripoli

Typically appearing more blue than green, the green heron may be seen in wooded wetlands throughout the state. Herons crouch, motionless, or slowly wade to hunt fish, frogs, snakes, and insects.
RICHARD DAY

67. LIME CREEK CONSERVATION AREA

Description: This county-owned park includes a restored prairie, several small ponds, and the Lime Creek Nature Center. Mammals here include white-tailed deer, red and gray foxes, and fox, red, and gray squirrels. Nesting birds include wood ducks, eastern screech owls, red-bellied woodpeckers, rose-breasted grosbeaks, and northern orioles. Several snakes, including fox snakes, are common.

Viewing Information: At the nature center, check out the wildlife displays. Watch the feeders for hummingbirds and rose-breasted grosbeaks in summer. In winter, the feeders attract black-capped chickadees, white-breasted nuthatches, and northern cardinals. Hike the trails in spring for wildflowers. In March and April, listen for displaying American woodcock on the prairie. The fall hawk migration is good from September through October. *USE CAUTION IN SOME AREAS DURING HUNTING SEASONS.*

Directions: *From the junction of U.S. Highways 18 and 65 in Mason City, follow US 65 (North Federal Avenue) north for 2.1 miles and turn east on Nature Center Road. Proceed 1 mile to the Nature Center. A map of the area is available at the center.*

Ownership: Cerro Gordo County Conservation Board (515) 423-5309

Size: 402 acres

Closest Town: Mason City

68. HAYDEN PRAIRIE STATE PRESERVE

Description: This tract of undisturbed native prairie is best known for its rich prairie plant diversity. Wildlife includes species that inhabit open prairie. Nesting birds include sedge wrens, yellow warblers, dickcissels, savannah and grasshopper sparrows, bobolinks, and eastern and western meadowlarks. The area also harbors a good diversity of butterflies. Mammals include red foxes and several species of rodents, such as the plains pocket gopher.

Viewing Information: The best way to see the area is to spend a few hours hiking the trails. Peak time to observe nesting birds is May and June. Northern harriers and upland sandpipers may occasionally nest here. Small mammals such as prairie voles and pocket gophers are common. Red foxes are sometimes seen. The butterfly watcher will find many prairie species here, from the spectacular regal and great-spangled fritillaries to the inconspicuous wild indigo and two-spotted skippers. The smooth grass snake is also resident. *THIS IS A STATE PRESERVE; ALL PLANTS AND ANIMALS ARE PROTECTED.*

Directions: *From the junction of U.S. Highway 63 and County Road A23 southwest of Lime Springs, follow CR A23 west 4.3 miles to a parking lot on the left, on the north edge of the prairie.*

Ownership: IDNR (319) 382-4895 or (515) 281-8676

Size: 240 acres

Closest Town: Lime Springs

69. CARDINAL MARSH WILDLIFE AREA

Description: This large wetland is located along the Turkey River and is one of most scenic in the northeastern Heartland. It is known for the spring migration of waterfowl, warblers, and other passerines. White-tailed deer, mink, red foxes, muskrats, and wild turkeys are residents. Nesting birds include pied-billed grebes, great blue herons, Canada geese, wood ducks, bobolinks, and yellow-headed blackbirds.

Viewing Information: The trees around the parking lot are excellent for migrant warblers, flycatchers, thrushes, vireos, and other passerines in May and September. On a good day, viewers may see 20 species of warblers. From the parking lot, follow the trail east along the dike, then follow the horse trail which loops south and eventually returns to the dike. This route skirts the marsh and passes through several grasslands and woodlots. The marsh is excellent for migrant waterfowl in March and April. As many as 15 species may be seen in a day. When water levels are low, large numbers of shorebirds are present, especially in May and August. These include lesser yellowlegs, solitary sandpipers, and common snipe. Watch for muskrats in the marsh and for mink along the marsh edge. The grasslands are home to nesting sedge wrens and bobolinks, with occasional sightings of red foxes. The wooded areas are home to nesting yellow-throated vireos, ovenbirds, rose-breasted grosbeaks, and wild turkeys. *USE CAUTION DURING HUNTING SEASONS.*

Directions: *From the junction of Iowa Highways 9 and 139 on the east edge of Cresco, follow IA 9 south for 0.4 mile and turn south on 345th Avenue. Proceed 2.5 miles and turn east on a gravel road that leads to a parking lot at the marsh.*

Ownership: IDNR (319) 382-4895

Size: 1,165 acres

Closest Town: Cresco

THE HEARTLAND

White-tailed deer are common throughout Iowa. The best time to view deer is at dawn or dusk, when they move toward forest openings. A loud snort and stomp of a hoof means the deer is alarmed; viewers should then move off a short distance.
DENVER BRYAN

REGION FOUR: THE NORTHEAST PLATEAU

The Northeast PaleozoicPlateau is Iowa's most rugged landscape. It contains deep, narrow valleys, limestone bluffs, rock outcroppings, and sheer cliff faces, plus karst topography features such as sinkholes, springs, and underground caverns. Within some cliffs, subterranean ice forms and remains throughout most of the summer. These cold-slope areas contain rare species such as the Iowa Pleistocene land snail and northern monkshood plant. Cold streams in the area contain Iowa's only naturally occurring brook trout populations.

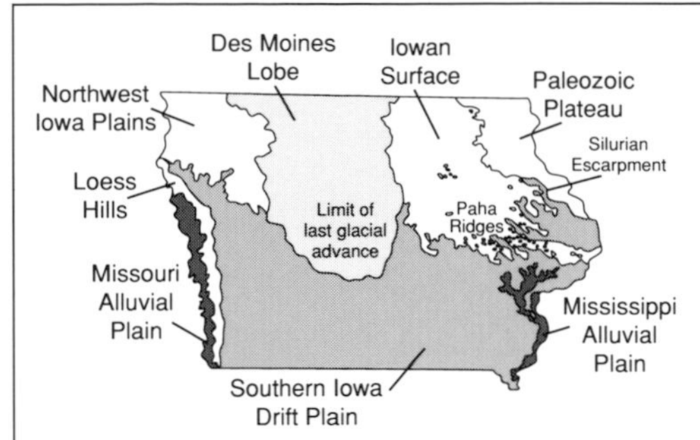

The poor soils and rugged terrain have helped reduce human impact in this area. This area was naturally more wooded than other parts of the state, thus some of the state's largest remaining woodlands and tracts of public land are found here. White oaks are frequently found on the ridgetops while red oaks grow on the slopes.

The Northeast contains a diversity of wildlife and is home to some of the state's rarest species. After being eliminated as a nesting species for more than 70 years, bald eagles returned first to this portion of the state to re-establish a nesting population. Peregrine falcons nested on the bluffs along the Mississippi River until the 1960s; and it is hoped they too will return. Pileated woodpeckers, red-shouldered hawks, and other sensitive species that require large tracts of habitat find adequate woodlands for nesting here. Wild turkeys, white-tailed deer, and ruffed grouse enjoy good populations here. Ducks, geese, tundra swans, bald eagles, ospreys, and many other species migrate along the Mississippi River.

Pikes Peak State Park.
CARL KURTZ

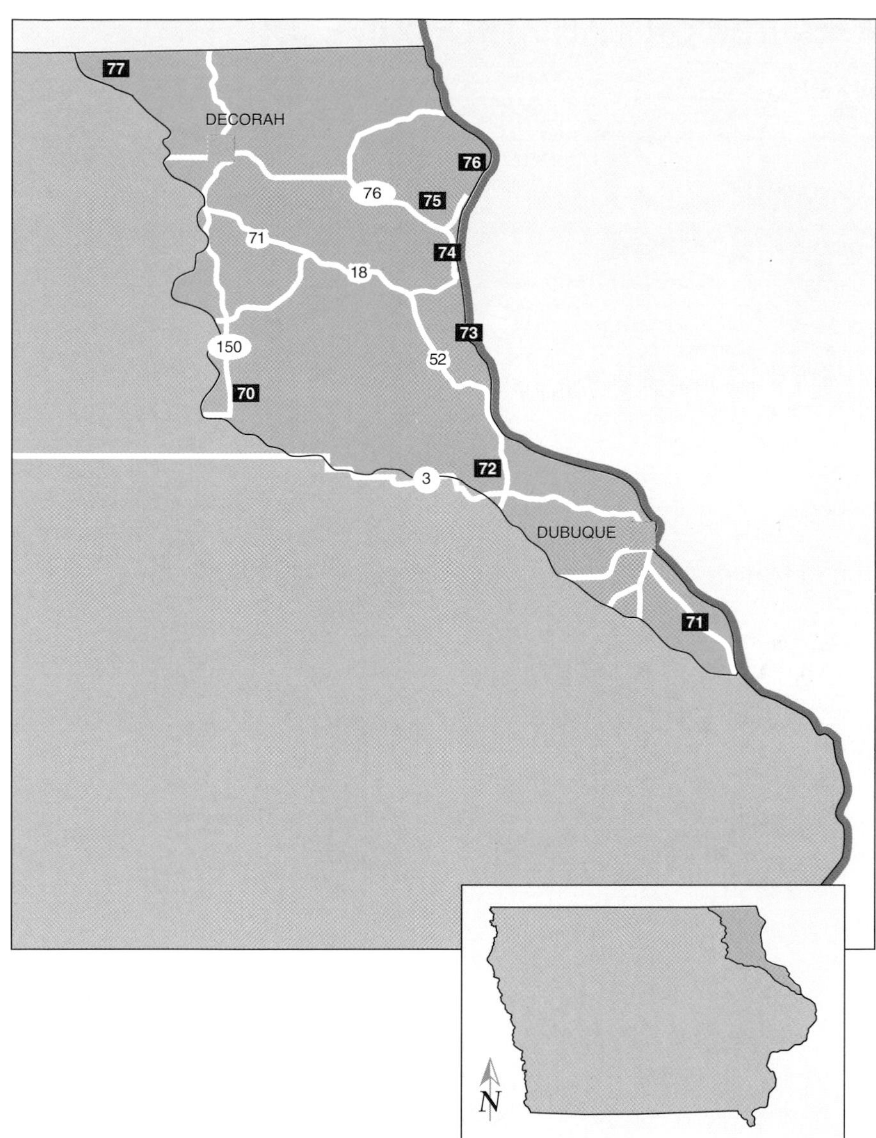

Wildlife Viewing Sites

70 Volga River Recreation Area
71 Mines of Spain Recreation Area
72 White Pine Hollow
73 Pikes Peak State Park
74 Effigy Mounds National Monument
75 Yellow River State Forest
76 Upper Mississippi Wildlife Refuge
77 Upper Iowa River Float Trip

RUGGED TERRAIN AND HIGH DIVERSITY

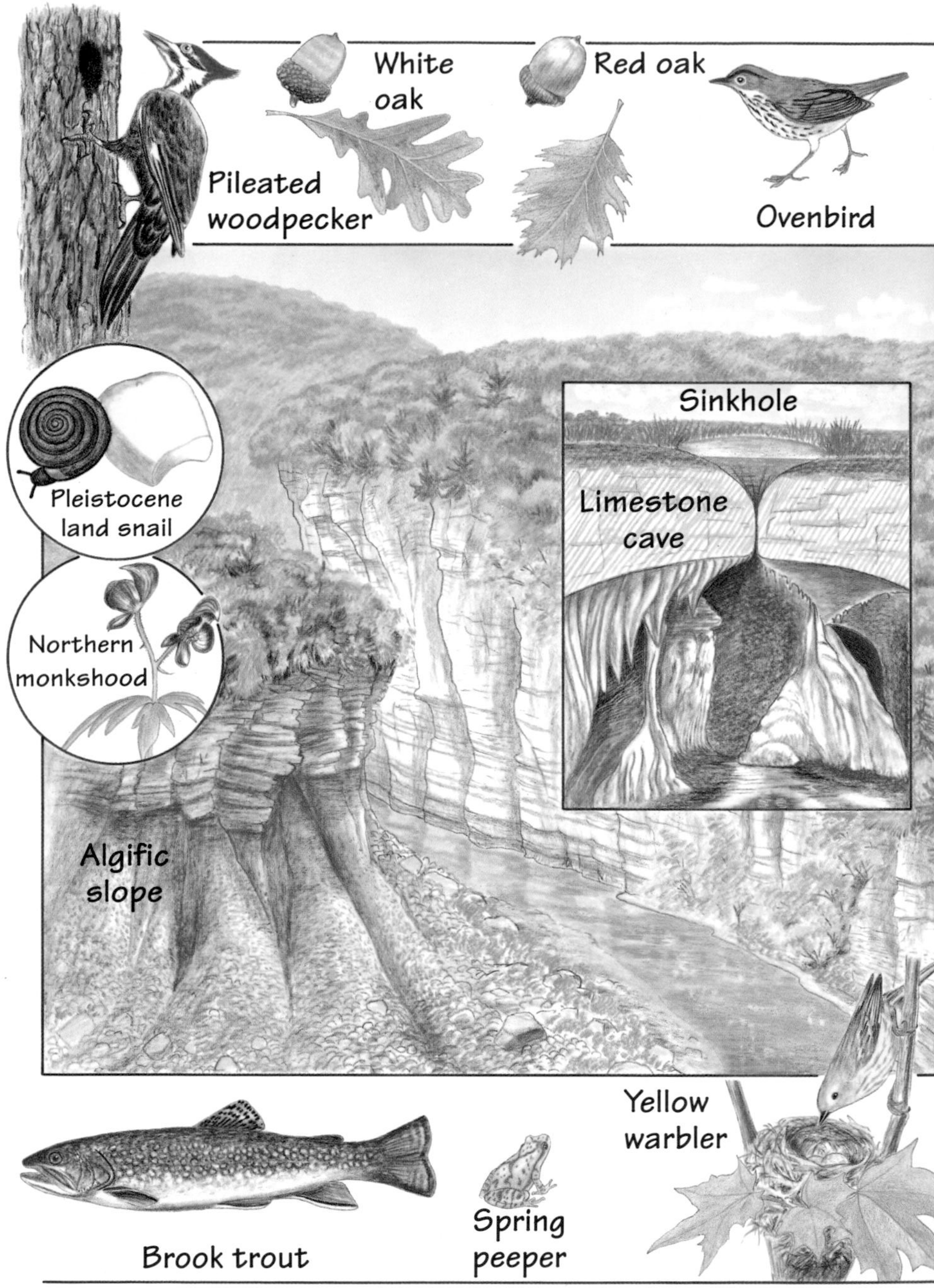

The rugged bluffs and fractured rock outcroppings of Iowa's Northeast Plateau are further riddled by dissolving rock minerals that create caverns, crevices, and sinkholes typical of karst topography. These subterranean-cooled slopes contain tiny, rare Pleistocene snails. Cold streams containing brook trout eventually drain into the Mississippi River. The bottomland forests of the river valley provide nest sites for prothonotary war-

blers, red-shouldered hawks, bald eagles, and heron colonies. The drumming of ruffed grouse can be heard in the spring. The large woodlands also support pileated woodpeckers, which will amaze visitors with their size. Winter visitors may occasionally cross the tracks of a bobcat in this rugged area. Interpretive centers are located at Sites 71 and 74. Site 73 has some boardwalk trails offering spectacular views of the Mississippi River.

70. VOLGA RIVER STATE RECREATION AREA

Description: This large, rugged area is heavily forested and features 135-acre Frog Hollow Lake. White-tailed deer, red foxes, mink, beavers, and wild turkeys are residents. Nesting birds include wood ducks, red-shouldered hawks, American woodcock, pileated woodpeckers, red-eyed vireos, and rose-breasted grosbeaks.

Viewing Information: The park contains 30 miles of trails, including a self-guided nature trail near the park office. Pileated woodpeckers are residents and are often seen around the lake and along the river. White-tailed deer are easily seen along forest edges throughout the area, except during fall hunting season. Weedy fields good for butterflies in summer, including tiger swallowtails. *USE CAUTION DURING HUNTING SEASONS.*

Directions: *From the junction of Iowa Highways 93 and 150 in Fayette, follow IA 150 (Lincoln Road) north 1.8 miles and turn east on Ivy Road. Proceed 1 mile and turn south at the "T" intersection into the area. A park map is available at the park office, immediately on the right past the entrance.*

Ownership: IDNR (319) 425-4161

Size: 5,420 acres

Closest Town: Fayette

71. MINES OF SPAIN STATE RECREATION AREA

Description: This tract of oak forest borders the Mississippi River and supports a rich diversity of wildlife, including wild turkeys, pileated woodpeckers, white-tailed deer, red and gray foxes, and river otters. Nesting birds include red-shouldered hawks, American woodcock, whip-poor-wills, ruby-throated hummingbirds, cerulean warblers, ovenbirds, and scarlet tanagers.

Viewing Information: Visit the E. B. Lyons Nature Center (open Monday through Friday, 9 a.m. - 4 p.m., year-round, and 12 p.m. - 4 p.m. on weekends from April 15 through October 15) to see wildlife displays, prairie flowers and a butterfly garden. Nearly 3 miles of paved roads and 8 miles of trails provide access to the area. Many nesting birds can be seen in the southern part of the park from Cattesse Hollow Access. Try viewing wildlife from a canoe on Catfish Creek. Bald eagles frequent the Mississippi River in migration and in winter. *USE CAUTION DURING HUNTING SEASONS.*

Directions: *From the junction of U.S. Highways 52/61/151 on the south side of Dubuque, follow US 52 south for less than 1 block and turn east on Bellevue Road. Proceed 0.5 mile to the E. B. Lyons Nature Center, on the left. A map of the area is available at the nature center.*

Ownership: IDNR (319) 556-0620

Size: 1,380 acres

Closest Town: Dubuque

72. WHITE PINE HOLLOW

Description: Named for its scattered groves of magnificent white pines, this preserve possesses the largest known stand of these trees in Iowa. North-facing talus slopes and cliffs contain cool, moist habitats that are inhabited by plants and wildlife typical of areas further north. About 90 species of birds summer here, including several raptors and species such as scarlet tanager, wood thrush, Acadian and great-crested flycatchers, pileated woodpeckers, and many warblers. In early spring, listen to the mesmerizing calls of whip-poor-wills. Lush ferns and beautiful wildflowers adorn wooded hillsides, especially in May.

Viewing Information: A poorly maintained access road on the east side of the preserve serves as a good hiking trail. Watch along it for white-tailed deer, wild turkeys, coyotes, red foxes, and gray squirrels. *SINCE SEVERAL ENDANGERED PLANTS AND ANIMALS ARE RESIDENTS, PLEASE TREAD LIGHTLY. USE CAUTION DURING HUNTING SEASONS.*

Directions: *From the intersection of Iowa Highway 3 and U.S. Highway 52 in Luxemburg, take IA 3 west for 2 miles. Turn north and follow the gravel road 1 mile to the preserve entrance.*

Ownership: IDNR (515) 281-8676

Size: 712 acres **Closest Town:** Luxemburg

73. PIKES PEAK STATE PARK

Description: This park offers breathtaking views of the Mississippi River valley from atop 500-foot-high bluffs. White-tailed deer and wild turkeys are residents. Nesting birds include great blue herons, bald eagles, ruby-throated hummingbirds, great-crested flycatchers, and cerulean warblers. Five-lined skinks can be observed during the warmer months.

Viewing Information: Explore the area via 13 miles of trails. In summer, check the hummingbird feeders at the concession area near the overlook—as many as a dozen ruby-throated hummingbirds may be seen here at once. Great blue herons and great egrets from nearby heron colonies inhabit the river in spring and summer. Bats are often seen near the shelter in summer. Enjoy fall colors and observe migrating raptors in September and October, including bald eagle and broad-winged and sharp-shinned hawks.

Directions: *From the junction of Iowa Highway 340 and U.S. Highway 18 Business Route in McGregor, follow IA 340 south for 1.9 miles and turn east on Pikes Peak Road (still IA 340). Proceed 0.4 mile to the park entrance. Bear left at the entrance to get to the overlook, where park maps are available at the kiosk by the restrooms.*

Ownership: IDNR (319) 873-2341

Size: 970 acres **Closest Town:** McGregor

74. EFFIGY MOUNDS NATIONAL MONUMENT

Description: This area contains mostly bottomland hardwood forest surrounded by wooded bluffs. Several remnant "goat prairies" can be found on the wooded bluffs. The area supports numerous ancient Indian burial mounds, dating back 2,000 years. Wild turkeys, white-tailed deer, red and gray foxes, beavers, and muskrats are residents. Nesting birds include Cooper's and red-shouldered hawks, yellow-bellied sapsuckers, pileated woodpeckers, wood thrushes, cerulean and prothonotary warblers, and scarlet tanagers.

Viewing Information: The park is open from sunrise to sunset only, and no picnicking is allowed. Visitor center hours are 8 a.m. - 5 p.m. daily, but it is open until 7 p.m. in summer. From the visitor center, hike the trails to the north along the bluffs for fantastic views of the Mississippi River valley, especially from Fire Point. Bird walks are held every other Saturday in summer and depart from the visitor center at 7 a.m. Expect to see blue-gray gnatcatchers, red-eyed vireos, cerulean warblers, ovenbirds, and scarlet tanagers. Wild turkeys and pileated woodpeckers have been seen here, and white-tailed deer are numerous. Both red and gray foxes are seen occasionally. Bottomland forest along the Yellow River is home to nesting wood ducks, red-shouldered hawks, yellow-bellied sapsuckers, American redstarts, and prothonotary warblers. The wildflower bloom is fantastic, with woodland species peaking late April through early May and prairie species peaking July through August. The September hawk migration can be excellent, with best viewing from Fire Point and other overlooks. Expect large numbers of turkey vultures, and broad-winged and sharp-shinned hawks at the peak. In winter, bald eagles are seen flying along the Mississippi River.

Directions: *From the junction of US 18 and Iowa Highway 76 in Marquette, follow IA 76 north 3.7 miles to the park entrance on the right.*

Ownership: NPS (319) 873-3491

Size: 1,475 acres

Closest Town: Marquette

P $

The wild turkey, peregrine falcon, greater prairie chicken, trumpeter swan, Canada goose, white-tailed deer, and river otter have all benefited from reintroduction programs in the state.

A TALE OF TWO RIVERS

Iowa is bounded by the nation's 2 longest rivers, the Missouri and the Mississippi.

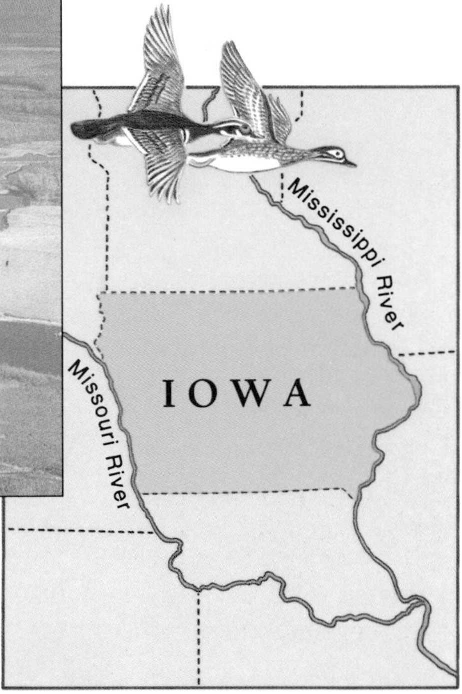

Mississippi River

IOWA

Missouri River

Since 1882, much of the Missouri has been converted into a fast flowing channel, and little of its natural wetland habitats remain. Waterfowl migrations are still impressive each spring and fall.

The Mississippi was first dammed in 1913. Now 26 locks and dams cross the river and have turned it into a series of pools. Wooded shorelines have been retained along much of the Mississippi, providing nesting habitat for many species. Bald eagles fish below the dams during the winter.

75. YELLOW RIVER STATE FOREST

Description: Steep limestone bluffs, deep valleys, coldwater trout streams, and mixed hardwood forests characterize this rugged area. Of several units, Paint Creek is the largest and most developed. The forest is home to ruffed grouse, wild turkeys, white-tailed deer, red and gray foxes, woodchucks, and several species of bats. Birds that nest here include Cooper's and red-shouldered hawks, whip-poor-wills, pileated woodpeckers, eastern phoebes, veeries, blue-winged, cerulean, and Kentucky warblers, ovenbirds, and scarlet tanagers. Rainbow, brook, and brown trout are stocked in Paint Creek.

Viewing Information: Viewing is from roads and more than 25 miles of trails in the Paint Creek Unit. White-tailed deer and wild turkeys are commonly seen, except during fall. Ruffed grouse can be heard drumming in April and May and reliably are seen in winter near the fire tower. Pileated woodpeckers commonly are seen year-round in the bluffs along Paint Creek. For several years, a hooded warbler has summered near the fire tower. Trails south and east of the fire tower pass through open fields and pine plantings where Cooper's hawks, American woodcock, blue-winged warblers, and field sparrows nest. The fall colors are spectacular here in October. *USE CAUTION DURING HUNTING SEASON.*

Directions: *From the junction of Iowa Highway 364 (Great River Road) and County Road B25 in Harper's Ferry, follow CR B25 southwest for 4.8 miles to the state forest boundary. Proceed another 1.5 miles to the headquarters, on the left.*

Ownership: IDNR (319) 586-2548, (319) 586-2254

Size: 7,687 acres

Closest Town: Harper's Ferry

Fall color peaks in October. Overlooks at Yellow River State Forest or along the Mississippi River provide excellent viewing of fall hawk migrations. The hawks soar on air currents created by major landforms. CARL KURTZ

76. UPPER MISSISSIPPI RIVER NATIONAL WILDLIFE AND FISH REFUGE

Description: This large refuge extends more than 260 miles along the Mississippi River in Iowa, Illinois, Minnesota, and Wisconsin. Pool 9 near Harper's Ferry is surrounded by floodplain forest and marsh and supports large numbers of waterfowl during migration. Tundra swans gather on the pool in fall. Bald eagles are also common, especially in late fall just prior to ice-up. Nesting birds include great blue herons, great egrets, wood ducks, red-shouldered hawks, barred owls, yellow-bellied sapsuckers, pileated woodpeckers, American redstarts, and prothonotary warblers. Mammals include beavers, muskrats, raccoons, mink, and white-tailed deer.

Viewing Information: Viewing is from roadsides. Since swans and other waterfowl may be distant, the use of binoculars or a spotting scope is necessary. Waterfowl peak from October through November, with diving ducks such as canvasbacks and lesser scaup predominating. Tundra swans peak in November, when 1,000 or more may be present. Bald eagles winter below Lock and Dam 9 and feed on fish within the pool while there is open water. In summer, look for double-crested cormorants, great blue herons, great egrets, wood ducks, ring-billed gulls, and prothonotary warblers. Ruffed grouse and pileated woodpeckers are occasionally seen along the road to the viewing area. *USE CAUTION IN SOME AREAS DURING HUNTING SEASONS.*

Directions: *The refuge visitor center is along U.S. Highway 18, 0.2 mile north of McGregor; pick up a map here. From the junction of County Roads B25 and X52 in Harper's Ferry, follow CR X52 (Great River Road) north for 2.6 miles and turn east on a gravel road. Proceed northeast for 0.5 mile to where the gravel ends. Weather permitting, continue another 0.2 mile to a point where you can see much of Pool 9 and the distant Lock and Dam 9 to the south.*

Ownership: USFWS (319) 873-3423

Size: 200,000 acres

Closest Town: McGregor

Five species of lizards live in Iowa. Some burrow more than 4 feet deep to hibernate during the winter. Skinks frequently lose their tails to predators, but can grow a new tail. Two of Iowa's skink species guard their eggs until hatching.

77. UPPER IOWA RIVER FLOAT TRIP

Description: One of the most scenic rivers in Iowa, the Upper Iowa River is home to a variety of wildlife. Much of the river passes through private property and the best way to see the area is by canoe. The 93-mile stretch from Lime Springs to the French Creek bridge is especially worth canoeing. The river passes through open farmlands into heavily wooded areas broken by steep limestone bluffs. White-tailed deer, beavers, mink, raccoons, and wild turkeys are all resident. Nesting birds include spotted sandpipers, belted kingfishers, bank swallows, yellow-throated vireos, indigo buntings, and northern orioles.

Viewing Information: Best viewing is by canoe from April to October, depending on water conditions. However, the lower portion may be viewed from County Road A26 in Allamakee County. In late fall and winter, this is a good area to view bald eagles, and an occasional golden eagle.

Directions: *Begin at Lidtke Park, on the west side of County Road V36 just north of Lime Springs. There are more than a dozen stopping points (including 3 in Decorah) along the 93 river miles to the French Creek bridge in Allamakee County. Write to the IDNR (Wallace State Office Building, Des Moines, IA 50319-0034) for information about canoeing the Upper Iowa River.*

Ownership: IDNR (319) 382-4895

Size: 93 river miles

Closest Town: Decorah

Iowa boasts 9,000 miles of floatable streams. The Upper Iowa River offers 93 miles of canoeing through scenic farmlands, wooded bluffs, and steep limestone cliffs. Watch for kingfishers, cliff and bank swallows, and, in late fall, bald eagles.

TOM TILL

WILDLIFE INDEX

The numbers following each entry are site numbers, not page numbers. The listing is divided by category of wildlife, and includes some of the more popular species in Iowa, helping you find some of the best places to see them. This is only a partial list.